Praise fo

M000195255

Retention: Key Mindsets That Retain Top Talent presents a unique and brilliant perspective on organizational culture and how it drives retention. Seldom have I seen such clarity around the employee experience and such a powerful solution to the retention problem. Bravo, Colene!

Steve Lowell, CSP
Author "Deep Thought Strategy"
Vice-President, Global speakers Federation

Colene's book is a must-read for employers and business owners who know they need help attracting and retaining today's workforce. This book focuses on taking your company to a career company; that rarefied air where every Sunday night, your employees look forward to coming to work. After reading this, you will invest time and energy in your employees and be rewarded with a happy workplace and increased profitably.

Roger Lear
President at OrlandoJobs.com
Co-Founder GreatInsuranceJobs.com
Pres. Lear & Assoc.

If you are a business leader who recognizes that your long-term success is directly linked to your ability to attract, equip, and most importantly retain your best and brightest, then Colene's book is for you. Highlighting the mutuality between employer and employee in all retention efforts, Colene has provided an engaging and practical guide that is the perfect balance of research, story-telling, and actionable content. This is a must read for all leaders!

Tony Moore, SHRM -SCP, SPHR
Speaker, Author and Culture Architect

These are challenging times, making thoughtful leadership paramount to successful business productivity and growth. Retention is an excellent guide, providing practical counsel for innovative leaders committed to developing a productive work culture and helping people achieve goals in work—and in life.

Diane McCain
Director of External Relations
Board of Governors
State University System of Florida

As an HR professional and former recruiter, Colene Rogers knows what companies must do to attract employees and, more importantly, how to keep them. Her insight into the 4 mindsets that employees operate from is very beneficial for any employer who wants to keep their most talented leaders and employees. A fresh and interesting take on a very important topic!

Jon Petz, CSP
Motivational Keynote Speaker and Conference Emcee

This is a must read for any manager or leader! Tales from the field, across multiple time periods and industries, make the insights in this book relatable and memorable. Everyone should aspire for their employees to take ownership of their jobs and Colene provides an easy to follow roadmap to turn your organization into the pinnacle "Career Company".

Heather "HD" Deyrieux, MSM, SHRM-SCP, SPHR
President
HR Florida State Council, Inc.

Without a doubt Colene is an inspirational and knowledgeable expert on talent acquisition and talent management including leadership, conflict management and best practices for supervisors. In her book Retention, Colene makes the case that employees who feel valued are less likely to quit and brings home the point that great leadership and the way you treat employees goes a long way towards preventing lawsuits. I highly recommend Retention and working with Colene Rogers.

Scott Callen
Partner
The Kullman Firm
Labor and Employment Law

Retention is spot on and reflects unique and well-thought-out solutions to finding, engaging and retaining talent. I highly recommend reading and implementing the advice given within. This message is consistent with our experience. The real value is working with Colene, as we have, to help identify, tease out the tough issues and incorporate the change necessary. Her touch and wisdom benefits the entire organization while coaching our managers responsible for leading our team. It's done on a continuum one opportunity to grow at a time.

Denver J. Stutler, Jr.
Chief Executive Officer
US Submergent Technologies

Retention: Key Mindsets That Retain Top Talent is a must read and will make you think differently about how you handle your recruitment and retention processes. Colene does an amazing job outlining the four mindsets of the employee life-cycle. The lessons shared in this book challenges leaders at all levels to reflect on their past experiences, encourages goal setting and building trust and character. With the use of short stories and antidotes, readers are guided through the phases of the employees' mindsets and retention architecture. This book could not have come at a better time!

Kara Palmer Smith
Senior Director, CareerSource Capital Region

Retention Key Mindsets That Retain Top Talent is a must read for leaders and managers who want to hire and retain high-performing team members. Most of us know and understand the high cost of turnover, but Colene Rogers takes us on a journey throughout this book that opens your eyes to not only the high cost of turnover and the lost opportunity cost of resources expended hiring replacement staff, but the intrinsic value of identifying, grooming, and cultivating top talent to remain with the company, realizing and recognizing each team member's value, and setting a goal to strive to be an Exclusive or Career Company. Colene effectively and creatively drives home the point that retention and cultivation of top talent is essential to long term success in business. Retention is truly one of the best books on human capital I have read in my 20+ year career as a leader and manager.

Terry L. Hill
Division Director at The Florida Bar,
President-elect of the National Association of Bar Executives (NABE)
President of the Florida State University College of Law Alumni Board of Directors.

RETENTI🔑N

KEY MINDSETS THAT RETAIN

TOP
TALENT

ColeneROGERS
THE TALENT KEEPER

HigherLife Development Services, Inc.
P.O. Box 623307 Oviedo, Florida 32762
(407) 563-4806
www.ahigherlife.com

© 2020 by Colene Rogers. All rights reserved.

No part of this book may be reproduced without written permission from the publisher or copyright holder, nor may any part of this book be transmitted in any form or by any means electronic, mechanical, photocopying, recording, or other, without prior written permission from the publisher or copyright holder.

Printed in the United States of America.

10 9 8 7 6 5 4 3 2 1   25 26 24 23 22 21 20

Rogers, Colene
Retention: Key Mindsets That Retain Top Talent

ISBN: 978-1-951492-97-7

Library of Congress case # 1-8510459161

Scripture taken from the Holy Bible, NEW INTERNATIONAL VERSION®, NIV® Copyright © 1973, 1978, 1984, 2011 by Biblica, Inc.® Used by permission. All rights reserved worldwide.

Contents

Contents

Introduction

In April 2019 a headline came across my phone:

*Unemployment 49-year low. Average
wage hits $27.77 an hour. April jobs
+263 K.*

I loved what I was seeing, so I clicked on the headline to read further.

A deeper look revealed that a record number of people in the workforce supported a steady increase in demand for goods and services, giving businesses little reason to cut staff, especially with skilled workers so hard to find. As early as 2019, open jobs exceeded the number of officially unemployed Americans by more than a million.

Then COVID-19 arrived and within a few short weeks, unemployment reached historic levels. 1. As of late April 2020, more than 33 million are unemployed for a real unemployment rate of 20.6%—which would be the highest level since 1934. At the time of this printing a staggering 26.5 million people have filed for unemployment.

Now, for me, an entrepreneur with a speaking, leadership training, and human resource (HR) consulting business, I know that periods of low and high unemployment are inevitable, and each situation brings unique challenges to my clients. I also know that in each situation employee retention is a critical component of business profitability and growth. During periods of low unemployment, the labor pool is small, which makes finding the right employee extremely challenging. When unemployment is high, the pool of qualified candidates to fill open positions is larger, and finding a qualified employee is easier. Employers find, however, one constant in both of these scenarios: turnover is expensive. Losing employees is costly, and the money lost would be better utilized to grow business, to boost profit, which in turns creates new jobs and opportunities. Regardless of unemployment data, employee retention is critical to a business's long-term success and growth.

My own experience confirms the same. From 2014 through 2017 I recruited for a Florida state-run agency and then a private engineering firm in Florida's panhandle. During those years, employers had an advantage over potential employees because there were fewer jobs than applicants to fill them; it was what I refer to as a buyer's market. Then the tide turned. Until the COVID-19 scare in early 2020, it was a seller's market because the employees who were selling their labor were considerably less in number than the amount of jobs employers needed to fill.

In my twenty years in the HR field, working in non-profit, in state government, in private sector companies, and now as a human capital consultant, I have found that many organizations struggle to attract, hire, and retain high value employees, regardless of unemployment numbers. It doesn't have to be that way though. Within the coming chapters I share principles to help you attract and retain your most valuable asset, your employees! The solutions I provide are not complicated or hard to understand, but they will not be simple or easy to implement. It will require an investment of time, energy, and resources. But most importantly, it will require heart—a genuine care and concern for your fellow man! Without heart, these solutions will be like a song sung without feeling, and few will want to listen. Apply them with sincerity, and your business can help you accomplish all your dreams.

A NEW BEGINNING FOR ME

In March of 2017, I left the engineering firm's HR department to begin my entrepreneurial career, establishing Colene Rogers and Associates, LLC. From that moment on I was 100 percent responsible for finding the business that would help make money for me and my family. I was way out of my comfort zone! But I believed the relationships I had made in Florida while serving as a member, vice-president, then president of the Big Bend Society of Human Resource Management (BBSHRM) and volunteering with the HR Florida State Council would generate opportunity and help me make the transition.

Quite soon after this, an HR colleague called and said she had an illness in her family and had been offered work she could not do. She asked if I would be interested. Even though it was not consultant work, I was glad and appreciative for the opportunity, being so recently out on my own.

The work was for ABC Company (a fictitious name). At an outdoor party for ABC employees, a female reported that one of the guys had inappropriate contact with her during a kickball game. With all the running around, coupled with the generous flow of alcohol, different interpretations of what exactly happened were provided. In her charge, she added that this was not an isolated incident, but rather a company-wide problem.

This was not the first time ABC had dealt with a sexual harassment case. In the past, they chose to settle other minor cases out of court, not as an admission of guilt, but to save money. I guess this situation got a little more of their attention because they brought me in to do an internal investigation to see if, in fact, they had a problem that went beyond this single event.

Over the next two months I went to eight different states, visited ten different branches, and interviewed forty-three employees comprised of men and women who were company managers, assistant managers, recruiters, and dispatchers. I then wrote and issued a report of my findings. Sitting with the CEO in his office, I told him I did not find evidence to support the charge that the company had a pervasive sexual harassment problem. I shared that I had met many wonderful people in his company and had gained their trust, which allowed them to open up and share their experiences with me. Then I said, "But, Mr. CEO, you do have an issue, which I'm sure you are aware of. You have very high turnover."

Of the forty-three people I interviewed for ABC, twenty-two were new hires, having been with the company for less than a year. One third of these new hires were supervisors, managers on the front line, the leaders who set the tone for all the other employees.

I asked the CEO for the opportunity to return another day to discuss the findings from my forty-three interviews because I could shed light on why people were leaving his company and recommend solutions. He agreed, and I was back within the week to speak to him and his colleague. As I described the situation, they both nodded their heads, agreeing with my assessment of the issues. Yet their nods seemed to be saying, *As a family-owned business, this is how we've done it for over four decades, and there is no need to change what has worked well for us.*

In the coming chapters I will show you why this backward facing or the "head-in-the-sand" approach does not work. Companies cannot ride the wave of yesterday's successes forever. Continued progress requires staying in step with changing markets and employee mindsets. After all, employees are your company's most valuable asset.

Part I

Employees' Mindset

Chapter 1

On Employee Mindsets and Their Importance

The same year I began my consultant business, my sister-in-law, Lori, moved to Tallahassee, Florida where my husband, Jim, and I live. The plan was for Lori to move here, and then have Jim and Lori's parents soon follow. Their parents had spent many wonderful years as retirees in beautiful Aiken, South Carolina, enjoying some of the best friendships of their lives. But almost all of those friends had moved to other communities, or sadly, passed away. They were now older, so having family nearby to provide companionship and care was something we were all interested in. There was nothing really keeping Lori in Indianapolis or Jim's parents in Aiken, so they both began taking steps to sell their homes and move south.

Lori first needed a place to work. For several years before her move she had worked in administration at a hospital in Indianapolis, Indiana. Not necessarily needing or wanting to stay in hospital administration, she came upon a job opportunity with a fine furniture store with several retail locations throughout Georgia.

She had been selling furniture on weekends to make extra money in Indianapolis, so this was not completely new to her. Her thought was to use this job to transition quickly to Tallahassee, get the lay of the land, and when the time was right, find a better opportunity.

After some positive online interaction with the company and a very good phone call with the man who would possibly hire her and be her supervisor, she came to Tallahassee for the in-person interview. She and her would-be boss clicked in the interview, and she learned the true earning potential of the job was much better than she originally thought. Lori began to see the job differently, as possibly more than just a temporary stop along the way. There was money to be made and positions she could pursue beyond the sales floor of the showroom, which is where she would start.

Lori was soon offered the job, and she accepted. With the confidence of having a job lined up, she gave notice to her employer in Indianapolis, sold her home, and officially moved to Tallahassee. It wasn't long before she was making the thirty-minute daily drive across the Georgia state line to sell fine furniture.

My experience has taught me that in employers' struggle with turnover and retention (they want to keep employees) many organizations fail to fully recognize what the majority of their employees actually think about working for them. From employee to employee, you may find all sorts and variations of perspectives, but when you consider the employees as a whole, a dominant mindset will emerge.

In Lori's story, she first thought of the furniture store as a temporary employment solution. It would serve the purpose of getting her to Tallahassee, and after her move, she would zero in on something more permanent. After the interview, though, her thinking shifted. She began to think the job had more long-term potential, seeing more financial opportunity and upward mobility.

Jim and I, being genuinely curious, would consistently ask Lori how things were going at the store. In the beginning, her feedback was mostly positive. She loved her boss! He was a great guy who went out of his way to help her. She was fitting in and her monthly sales numbers were always increasing.

But after about a year's time, her thinking had changed. When you've worked someplace for a year you become quite familiar with the quality of the whole employee experience. Lori learned that retail hours can really get in the way of her life outside the job, and the company didn't always assist in her efforts to get away from work when there was something important for her to do. As nice and helpful as her boss was, he didn't always address personality issues brought on by one or two difficult employees who were negatively affecting the entire sales team. These examples (and more) had her again viewing the company as a temporary employment solution. Fast forward one more year and her experience had grown more negative. When asked about the job she would say, "I just don't want to be there anymore." Six more months passed by, and she moved on.

Lori is only one employee's experience among several other employees at the furniture store. But you can be sure that there are shared positive and negative experiences among employees that determine how the majority perceive the organization, the dominant mindset. There is always a dominant mindset that reveals if the majority of an organization's employees plan to stay with their company or leave it quickly. If you can discover the dominant mindset in your organization then you can make changes that will substantially lower your turnover rate, which boosts your profit.

THE FOUR MINDSETS

In my work with ABC Company and several other companies as a consultant, combined with the years I have spent as an HR employee, I have identified four mindsets that reflect the level of commitment that a majority of employees have about an organization. And that level of commitment is what drives them to ask the question, *Do I still want to work here?* An employee who loves everything about their job, may not ever ask themselves that question. An employee who finds very little to like about their job may ask themselves that question multiple times a day.

INSIGNIFICANT

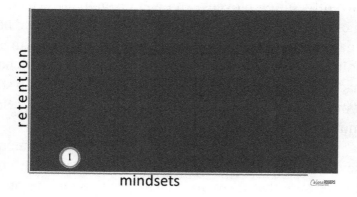

The first mindset is what I call *Insignificant.* This means the majority of employees believe the company is a difficult place to work; they don't hold their position or the company in very high regard, and they quickly start looking for another employment opportunity.

If most of your employees have a mindset of *Insignificant*, this is what you'll see:

- Your turnover rate is higher than the average for your industry.
- People leave your organization without another job already lined up.
- You don't have enough employees to do the work.
- You rely heavily on the employees you have. Employees are always being asked to do more, work longer shifts, and work harder.
- You're constantly shuffling people around where they are needed to cover the work. You might have employees doing jobs they weren't really hired to do, but this cannot be helped because the work has to get done.
- When people come into the organization they typically don't stay very long. Operations and relationships are so stressed by the lack of people to do the work that it creates an environment that people want out of quickly.
- You find employees don't give the typical two-week notice. They show up one day and say this is my last day, or they just stop showing up altogether and never even let you know.
- The level of talent is relatively low in your organization because the "A players," those highly talented individuals, rarely stay for very long, or they don't accept a job offer in the first place.

• New people are always coming in to replace those who have left, and they are forced to get up to speed very fast, often without proper training. It naturally follows that you have to go back and redo work that wasn't done right the first time.

• You ask employees to train the newly hired, on top of all the work they are already being asked to do.

• Employee referrals are almost non-existent. If you do receive referrals the applicants are often not very qualified.

• Potential job candidates might not show up for a scheduled interview, and new hires might not even show up on the first day.

• You are in constant need of employees, and this puts you at a huge disadvantage with your competition. Therefore, you feel like you need to hire anyone with a pulse.

• Supervisors think twice about terminating poor performing employees because the need for workers creates an overall lowering of standards.

• You might have business booked in advance, and you're not sure how you're even going to get it done, but you will cross that bridge when you get there.

• For supervisors, time away from the company can be hard to justify because the business is so dependent on them.

Businesses with an *Insignificant* dominant mindset can stay open for a while, but unless they can make changes that will positively influence the way their employees think about them, it is going to be very difficult to stay in business.

TEMPORARY

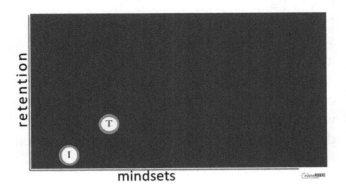

The second mindset is what I call *Temporary*. This means that the majority of employees think the company is an okay place to work, but it is only a stepping-stone to something better.

If most of your employees have a *Temporary* mindset you will see:

- Your turnover is average for your industry.
- You might even look at this turnover rate and say we are about the same as everybody else, so this is normal. There's is nothing we can do about it.
- You have just enough employees to get the job done. For example, let's say you have a project where four people would be best, but three people can get it done, you have three.
- Any unexpected decrease in available employees to do the work can leave you short staffed until you can fill those positions.

• You're not growing as much as maintaining your market share, so most of your recruiting is to replace employees who left rather than recruiting for newly created positions.

• As soon as you fill one position another seems to open up, and there can be several to fill at one time.

• Keeping high-tech positions filled is a constant worry in the back of your mind because no one else in your company can do what they do. It can take time to find a qualified person who is the right fit, so high-tech job vacancies can really cost you.

• Supervisors who are desperate to fill much needed positions pay more visits than usual to HR pushing them to do everything in their power to find qualified replacements. If someone isn't found soon you might even have to hire an independent contractor to do the work for you.

• In high demand times, you might hire workers from temporary staffing agencies to help get the job done.

• Your employees stay for a while to gain experience and develop, but over time they discover more and more reasons to leave and find another place of employment.

• You get some employee referrals which helps you fill some of your open positions.

• Because it's all-hands-on-deck, all the time, job training can suffer, and you're almost forced to give employees tasks they aren't completely ready to take on. They might say, "I've never done this!" but they are told to do their best to figure it out and ask another person for help if they need it.

• Without a surplus of employees, there is little time to pursue new initiatives or address issues in an effective way.

• Supervisors might lower performance standards for employees because they are afraid to offend them and give them a reason to leave. It's like the employees are calling the shots, and you feel somewhat beholden to them.

• The business is very dependent on its supervisors, so they have to work long hours. If a supervisor does get time away from the business, they have to stay in constant contact with the company because there isn't anyone else who has the knowledge to truly cover for them.

Businesses with a *Temporary* dominant mindset can survive and do okay. Some organizations remain at this mindset level throughout the entire life of the business. But *Temporary* organizations tend to plateau and never reach their full potential.

Companies that currently have a *Temporary* dominant mindset can and should strive to move ahead to the next mindset, which is pivotal. To reach the next mindset means an important change has started to take place for your company. Here, employees and applicants are beginning to think of you as a long-term employment solution. But one reason many organizations struggle to move beyond a *Temporary* mindset is because of an underlying belief held by many employees, especially true of the younger generation, that they aren't going to work anywhere for any great length of time. As a result, organizations buy into the same belief, which negatively affects the level of effort they are willing to invest to retain employees. Thus, this belief can become a sort of self-fulfilling prophecy. Companies should carefully guard against this belief because the move from *Temporary* to the next mindset is a shift that propels companies to experience a substantial increase in their retention rate.

EXCLUSIVE

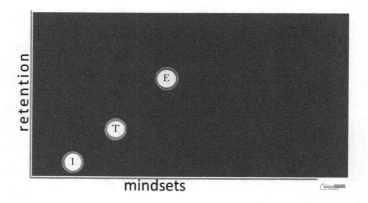

I call this third mindset *Exclusive*. To be an organization viewed by the majority of employees as *Exclusive* means that most employees think the company is a good place to work, and they have no plans to leave anytime soon because many of their wants and needs are being met.

If most of your employees have an *Exclusive* mindset you will see:

- Your turnover rate is better than your industry average.

- You have enough employees to do the job and then some. Let's say you have a project that requires a minimum of three people to do the work. You have four.
- For the most part, you are able to handle the occasional unexpected departure of some employees because you are pretty well staffed.
- You don't have to ask too much of your employees, and this helps create a less stressful working environment.
- Plenty of companies want to lure your employees away, especially your "A players," so you feel the pressure to keep them engaged and satisfied.
- Your business is growing, which is good, but with that comes the pressure of staying well-staffed with talented employees.
- Because you have more employees than the bare minimum, some employees can concentrate their efforts on gaining new customers, creating new products, or developing better systems.
- Employees typically enjoy working here, so you get enough qualified referrals to help keep your positions filled.
- You can be more selective in who you hire because you have qualified candidates interviewing for jobs, and being you're well-staffed gives you a little breathing room.

Businesses with an *Exclusive* dominant mindset can continue to do well and grow, but growth brings other challenges, so companies at this mindset have to stay on their "A game."

CAREER COMPANY

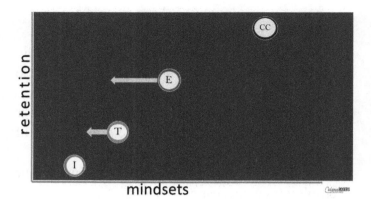

The fourth and final mindset is even better than *Exclusive*, but only a few companies will ever get there. This is the *Career Company* mindset. At this top level, the majority of employees think the company is a great place to work, and they can't see themselves working for anyone else. This is the mindset companies want their employees to have.

If most of your employees have a *Career Company* mindset you will see:

• Your employee retention rate is the envy of companies inside and outside of your industry.
• There is a culture of excellence and achievement that creates an environment where the less ambitious feel out of place and might even leave. The employees who do leave are mostly those who retire or the ones you want to leave.
• You're always well-staffed with talented employees.

- Many of your upper- and lower-level supervisors have been with the company for several years. They provide a wealth of experience and knowledge and mentorship for emerging leaders.
- There is a line of referrals, each one hoping he is chosen to fill an open position when it becomes available.
- Many talented and qualified candidates are always sending in their resumes, so you have a waiting list of great candidates. The result is that when positions open up, they don't remain open for very long.
- When new hires come on board, they already see you as a long-term solution for employment, a place they could spend their entire career. This makes negotiations with new hires rather easy and efficient.
- A surplus of experienced employees who possess lots of knowledge allows you to train your staff effectively. This gives employees even more reasons to stay.
- There is plenty of upward mobility opportunity because the company is always growing.

FOR FURTHER REFLECTION

In this first chapter, we've identified the four dominant mindsets and their characteristics. Before we move ahead, let's begin discerning your employees' current dominant mindset. Reflect for a few minutes on why your employees perceive your company as they do, and how you can shift their mindset from *Insignificant* or *Temporary* to *Exclusive* or *Career Company*.

1. Reflect back over your career and identify the mindsets of companies you have worked for. What factors contributed to their having that mindset?

2. What would you say is the dominant mindset of your company?

3. What is the first thing your organization can do to raise the mindset level in the eyes of applicants and employees?

Chapter 2

Employee Life Cycle

I know the question you are asking now is this: *What will it take for my company to become a Career Company in the minds of our employees?* To answer this, we must look at what I describe as the *Two-Stage Life Cycle* that every employee goes through during their journey from new hire to a productive member of your organization. The two stages of this cycle are what I define as the *Integration* and *Ownership* stages. Then the *Employee Engagement Environment*, the culmination of employees' experiences throughout the *Two-Stage Life Cycle*, reveals which of the four mindsets your employees perceive your company to be.

THE INTEGRATION STAGE

My *Two-Stage Life Cycle* begins with the *Integration* stage. *Integration* is the process by which an employee becomes a part of the living network of people you call a company. First, the company and the new employee must first find one another. Whether this is initiated by the company or the employee, either way the employee is made aware of a job opportunity.

Next the company and the employee start getting to know one another. The employee visits the company's website to learn about the organization; they watch videos that introduce the company's culture to potential job applicants; they go to Glassdoor to learn about the company's reputation; they fill out an online application, and they go through the interview process, which is made up of some mix of phone, online, and in-person meetings. Finally, a job offer follows, which can involve a negotiation of salary.

The first day of work arrives, and typically, the employee is not asked to do much. Forms are filled out; they are shown their desk, cubicle, or work station; they learn where everything is and how everything flows; they are taken around and introduced to the people they will work closely with and introduced to others they won't; they might be taken out to lunch; they read manuals, watch software tutorials, and learn what is expected of them and how to do it. Then, more and more, with each passing day they perform the job they were hired to do.

Outward events are not the only activities taking place in the *Integration* stage. Inward actions are just as busy: the employee is in the process of finding their place, fitting in, getting to know the people they work with, identifying the top performers, the big personalities, learning the leadership style of their supervisor, learning if they like their supervisor and what kind of relationship they can hope to have with them, finding the people they relate to and those they don't, exploring future options and paths of upward mobility. In essence, they are getting to know the company and the company is getting to know them.

The time it takes to complete the *Integration* stage is different for everybody, but at some point, the employee becomes fully integrated. They no longer see themselves as the new guy or the new girl, but rather as a contributor whose skill level matches that of their team members. They are an equal player who has proven themselves.

THE OWNERSHIP STAGE

The employee now enters the second stage of the *Two-Stage Employee Life Cycle*. This is the *Ownership* stage. Here a relationship between the employee and the company forms and develops, so that now in the employee's mind, they are a part of the company and internally believe, "This is my company."

To illustrate, my husband, Jim, plays electric guitar for our church praise band. The Sunday morning call time for the band is seven thirty, and by that time they want band members plugged in, tuned up, and ready to rehearse a final run through of the four-song set before the first of three services begins. Jim happened to arrive early one particular Sunday and found himself alone in the sanctuary as he was setting up his guitar rig. Probably inspired by the fact that no one else was there, a thought in the form of a question came to him: *What if I was responsible for making sure everything goes off without a hitch this morning?* With that, he began to look beyond his guitar duties. He removed some music and microphone stands from the platform left behind after Wednesday night's rehearsal. He turned on the lights in the wings so the musicians who would soon arrive could better see, and he braced the doors open, so arrivals wouldn't need to set down their guitars and amps to open them. Jim was taking ownership.

When an employee takes ownership, they start to question the current reality of their job from two perspectives. The first is from the perspective of what is best for the company. Now that they are familiar with the mission, strategies, processes, and culture of the company, how can they do their part to improve operations? How can they help the company do what it does even better? When an employee takes ownership, they develop a keen eye and ear to identify opportunities and detect trouble.

The second is from the more personal perspective of what is best for them. How can they arrange work to work better for them? Can they be creative with the hours they work? Can they work some from their home? What new skills can they acquire through the company to increase their value to the organization and beyond?

With their developing sense of ownership and their knowledge and ability growing, the employee now possesses a confidence in their own competence that can make them a more assertive employee. They are more likely to pursue leadership roles and speak out; to look for new tasks and challenges; to identify areas where they think they can make a difference.

Several years ago, I went to work in the HR department for a quasi-state agency in Florida. I was hired as an HR generalist, but once I became integrated I realized our recruiting process was old and antiquated. We were not using many available current resources to attract and hire the best talent. I asked my supervisor if I could take on revising our recruitment process, and she said yes. It wasn't long before I was spending the majority of my days managing new talent recruitment for the entire agency.

I stopped using our local newspaper as a way to advertise our job openings, with its limited reach and very expensive ads, and also stopped using financial periodicals where our job ads would be old news by the time they were released. I then purchased recruiter seats on LinkedIn and Indeed. We immediately began getting a greater number of candidates, filling our positions faster with more talented individuals. All because our new ads were seen by candidates all across the world while our previous ads were more local and regional in reach.

THE EMPLOYEE ENGAGEMENT ENVIRONMENT

When the employee first made contact with the company, they entered into the *Employee Engagement Environment*. This environment consists of the totality of everything they experience as an employee in both the *Integration* and *Ownership* stages of the life cycle and the power of those experiences to either engage or disengage them. Recall that I have identified four mindsets that reflect the level of commitment that the majority of employees have about an organization. And it is that level of commitment that drives them to ask themselves the question *Do I still want to work here?* The quality of the *Employee Engagement Environment* is the determining factor in how the majority of your employees answer that question. I repeat. The quality of the *Employee Engagement Environment* is the determining factor in how the majority of your employees answer the question, *Do I still want to work here?* And the answer they give determines whether they think of your company as *Insignificant, Temporary, Exclusive,* or a *Career Company.*

Your employees started evaluating everything in the engagement environment even before you had your first contact with them. They were evaluating the quality of the website; the mission and values expressed on the website; the video that introduced your company culture; the comments about your company on Glassdoor and your overall online reputation; the phone interactions to set up the interviews; the personalities of the people who interviewed them and the questions they asked; the ease of salary and benefit package negotiations; your products and services; your involvement in the community; the onboarding process (or the lack of one); the type of people they work with; the relationship with their supervisor (or the lack of one); the quality of training; the opportunities for advancement and upward mobility; the leadership opportunities; the team experience; the quantity and quality of recognition; the quality of the technology; the quality of all the equipment; the creative opportunities; the quality of performance feedback; the work/life balance; the business hours of operation; the pay, and more.

Each one of your employees is unique, so what is important to one employee from the above list won't necessarily be important to the next. But here is the thing: all this evaluating is leading up to a decision. If the *Employee Engagement Environment* has been healthy and supportive; if the employee has had a positive experience during the *Integration* stage; if, in the *Ownership* stage their assertiveness and initiative was encouraged; if their boss took a sincere interest in helping them reach their goals; then the employee is likely to commit to the company and stay. That doesn't mean they will stay forever. There will always be potential exit points in the future. But for now, the company is meeting their needs and they want to work there.

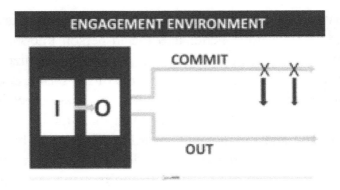

If the engagement environment has been unhealthy and more of a negative experience; if they never fully integrated because they never felt like they fit in; if all of their initiative and assertiveness in the *Ownership* stage was met with resistance and discouragement, being told to just do the job they were hired to do; if their supervisor never took the time to get to know them; if this and more happened, it is likely that at some point they will decide to leave. They may not leave right away, but they are now ready for a better opportunity to present itself. And when they make that decision it is too late; their mind is made up, and there is very little you can do to change it.

And the reality is that this is a decision we don't even see because all their thoughts and perceptions about the organization are completely hidden. Without a mechanism to discover what the employee is thinking, the supervisor will say, "I never saw it coming," when a top performer or emerging leader decides to leave.

A close friend recently left a job for what she thought was going to be a great opportunity. In this new job she would once again get to use her interior design skills, for which she had a degree and previous experience. I was excited for her, especially when she told me about her interview with the owner and CEO! The phone interview couldn't have gone better and the in-person interview went the same. She described him as very organized, able to talk about the different facets of the business in clear, concise, and detailed fashion. He was direct in the interview, which is a quality she likes having in a supervisor, and she looked forward to working for him.

So I was both shocked and saddened when a month later, over a taco salad, she told me that the guy was a control freak who demanded—in abusive tones—employees to do things his way. He spared no one. Sitting there over lunch it was obvious she doubted this position was going to work.

A week later, after only five weeks on the job, she texted me to say she was going in that morning to resign first thing. Later she recounted what happened. In his office, she could tell by the expression on his face that he was surprised at what he was hearing, but he made no attempt to change her mind. Even if he had, it wouldn't have mattered. She was way past the point of giving the job another chance. You know it was bad because she left without having another job lined up, something she had never done before. The leadership style and skills of a company's managers and supervisors are a determining mindset factor. My friend's boss created such a negative environment that her mindset quickly changed from *Exclusive* to *Insignificant,* and she wanted out. A boss without effective leadership skills can harm a company's ability to grow and thrive, which is a critical element of the *Employee Engagement Environment.* The *Silo Affect* is another occurrence that negatively influences an engagement environment.

THE SILO AFFECT

If you're like most companies, when you hear about the four mindsets with their symptoms, you identify with one of the first three, but you're pretty certain you have not reached *Career Company* status in your employees' minds. For this, you might be tempted to blame a booming economy that gives the advantage to the employee over the employer. Or maybe your industry has an average rate of turnover that is high, so you're resigned to the idea that there is nothing you can really do about it. Perhaps you believe the world has forever changed and career companies are a thing of the past. Those explanations, and others like them, are truly only excuses that prevent positive change.

Most organizations have an organizational chart that depicts the hierarchy and flow of command that is unique to their organization. It is not uncommon to find these three operational groups on any given company organizational chart: the highest-ranking executives often referred to as the C-Suite (CS), Human Resources (HR) and Supervisors (S). Each of these operational groups has duties that it alone is responsible for, and when combined with the other groups, complete every task to be carried out by the company. A good amount of coordination between all three is required for top performance, but what often happens is they begin to work in silos, growing independent of each other, and operating out of sync with one another.

The ability to acquire and retain talent is not just one issue among many that organizations must deal with, it is *the* issue! Without competent employees to fill all your positions, it is going to be very hard to win.

And without a coordinated effort, companies will lack an effective turnover prevention strategy, never going beyond *Temporary* or *Exclusive* in the minds of their employees.

ABC COMPANY REVISITED

Let's revisit the story of ABC Company from the Introduction. They had a very high turnover problem. When over half of the people I interviewed had been with the company for less than a year, that is a problem.

Those forty-three people I spoke with basically told me that the *Employee Engagement Environment* was not healthy or supportive. The management style of some of the leaders at the corporate office was authoritative and could be confrontational and contentious. Senior leaders were known to yell and cuss at the managers.

Branch managers complained of a lack of transparency because they were being kept in the dark on matters they believed to be important. For example, personnel were sometimes fired at one branch without other branches ever being notified about the firing or given the reason why.

There was such a feeling of distrust that some employees were afraid to pursue higher positions in the company because those supervisors didn't seem to last. In their minds, they perceived more job security staying right where they were.

Some managers felt that corporate didn't "have their back," saying corporate would take the side of customers when there were disagreements or issues with the customer.

The poor engagement environment created, at best, a *Temporary* mindset among ABCs employees. When employees asked themselves, *Do I still want to work here?* Their answer was, *No, not for very long.* The employees would come in and quickly realize they wanted out, or they would decide to stay but only until something better came along. ABC spent thousands of dollars attracting, hiring, and training talent only to have many of them leave.

About a year ago, I received a letter from their accounting department where I saw the company had been bought out. This was a family run business that was established forty-five years before. Without an effective turnover prevention strategy, ABC was not able to retain their most valuable asset, their people. If they had, ownership of the company might still be in the hands of the family.

RETENTION ARCHITECTURE

What any company needs to achieve a *Career Company* status in the minds of their employees is a *Retention Architecture*. *Retention Architecture* delivers five desired outcomes:

- Find and hire qualified candidates to fill all of your positions.
- Create trusted leadership within the organization.
- Resolve conflict in a timely and effective manner.
- Increase employee engagement.
- Strengthen HR practices to keep you out of court.

In addition to the five desired outcomes, a company's

Retention Architecture gives the entire organization a coordinated turnover prevention strategy. It strengthens the *Employee Engagement Environment* by giving employees a positive and engaging experience, moving them ever closer to a *Career Company* mindset. It gives employees, who have decided to stay with your company, more reasons to stay in the future when they face possible exit points. And do you remember the belief held by many employees that they will never work anywhere for any great length of time, which companies tend to buy into? The *Retention Architecture* works to reverse that belief.

FOR FURTHER REFLECTION

Now the elements that shift companies to an *Exclusive* or a *Career Company* dominant mindset are growing clearer. From the first moment a potential employee engages with your company, whether online or in person to being hired and becoming a valued employee, consider what impression your company makes. Answer the following questions about your company's *Employee Engagement Environment*.

1. What do you think is the first impression job applicants have when they are introduced to your company? Is that impression a lasting one?

2. Does your company encourage employees to be assertive and take ownership of the organization?

3. What does employee engagement mean to you? What successes has it led to in your organization?

4. What changes can be made to your team, department, or company that would make the *Employee Engagement Environment* a more positive one?

Chapter 3

Employees' Power of Choice

W hen an employee chooses to leave an organization, they do so because they believe they will benefit in some way. Here are some of the possible benefits: more pay and a better benefits package; perform work more to their liking; the opportunity to add new skills and experience to their resume; chase a new adventure; live in a new geographical area. Whatever the reason might be, employees typically make choices for something they want that they think will be better for them.

On the other hand, their choosing to leave always comes at a cost to the employer. Because employees have the power of choice, it is up to employers to give them reasons to stay.

However, it is important to understand that some of the reasons employees choose to leave are beyond your control. No matter how great of a place your company is to work, you can't compete with the restlessness of youth, the desire to be closer to family, or the inclination to change direction in life.

My youngest son recently graduated from Florida State University (FSU), and we hosted a gathering of friends and family at our home to celebrate the occasion. During the celebration, one of my son's good friends, shared that he would soon be moving to Utah. He graduated from FSU a year and a half before my son and immediately landed a job in banking at a credit union in Tallahassee. He was enjoying much success there, managing up to twenty-to-thirty people at a time. Impressive for a young man! But with a sister in Utah and the strong desire for a change, he gave notice to his company letting them know he would be leaving in January of 2020. He liked his job, but there was nothing his company could have done to keep him. He wanted a life change.

THE COST OF TURNOVER

In a past position, I recruited for a private company. Skilled engineers, field technicians, and a knowledgeable sales staff were all required to deliver our product and service. When these positions became vacant, the pressure was on to fill them quickly because we had contracted work to do along with new job contracts we wanted to pursue. But filling those positions could take time, typically two-to-six months for our company. We had to be patient to find the right person for the job. If the weeks started to add up with no good candidate in sight, managers would start to frequent my office and earnestly ask how the search was going for replacements. With the clock ticking, it could get a little testy as we tried to fill that empty seat. Before I came the company would often have to go outside the company and pay a premium to get the skilled workers we needed to do the job.

In his article, "The Hidden Costs of Turnover,"

Bob Rodgers says, "The cost of losing and replacing a strategic or critical employee starts at 150 percent of the value of that employee's compensation package." If you have an employee whose salary and benefits package totals a hundred thousand dollars, your cost will start at a hundred fifty thousand to replace him.

Josh Bersin of Deloitte estimates that the cost of losing an employee ranges from tens of thousands of dollars to 150 to 200 percent of that employee's annual salary.

In a more comprehensive study from the Center for American Progress, which consisted of eleven different research papers over fifteen years, found that "the average economic cost to a company of turning over a highly-skilled job is 213 percent of the cost of one year's compensation for that role."

MY TURNOVER CALCULATOR

In my work with clients, I use a seventy-five-line-item *Turnover Calculator* I created, based on research from the United States Department of Labor and the Society of Human Resource Management. With this calculator I am able to determine the cost of turnover for any position in the company.

There are two main cost categories, the hard costs and the soft costs. The hard costs are those associated with separation, vacancy, replacement, and training. The soft costs pertain to the lost productivity when an employee leaves your organization. What I have found is that many companies don't factor in the lost productivity associated with losing talent.

Here are some line item examples from the *Turnover Calculator*:

HARD COSTS OF TURNOVER
Pre-Departure Separation Costs

- Exit interview staffing costs
- Payout of annual leave
- Other separation costs (unemployment benefits)

Vacancy Costs

- Temporary and contract workers
- Coworker burden (overtime, added shift)

Replacement Costs

- Search costs: advertising
- Criminal history and driving record
- Staff prep and actual interviewing time
- Orientation costs

Training Costs

- External training
- On-the-job training

SOFT COSTS OF TURNOVER
Pre-Departure Separation Costs

- Lost productivity of departing employee
- Lost productivity of supervisor

During Vacancy Costs

- Lost productivity of vacant position
- Lost productivity of supervisor

Selection and Sign-On Costs

- Lost productivity of coworkers
- Lost productivity of supervisor

There are other intangible costs that cannot be measured by the *Turnover Calculator*:

- The dip in morale when you lose a top performer or a beloved supervisor.
- The stress on workers who cover the work of an employee who left and its effect on engagement and productivity.
- The loss of faith in the organization among existing employees when there is a high rate of turnover.
- The damage to the company's online reputation when turnover is high.
- Increased performance error rates due to less experienced employees, with the potential to harm customer relationships.

Get an excel spreadsheet to determine the cost associated with losing your talent at ColeneRogers/turnover.com.

LAYING THE FRAMEWORK

In his post "How much does turnover really cost?" Jack Altman makes the point that employee turnover is expensive, but most people have no framework for quantifying this cost, or never even bother to try. And without knowing the cost impact on their business, they don't take employee retention seriously enough.

He goes on to draw an analogy between smoking and turnover. As far back as the 1920s, people were becoming aware that cigarettes were bad for a person's health. Despite that, the number of Americans who smoked continued to increase. Then in 1964, the first Surgeon General's Report on Smoking and Health came out that linked smoking to heart disease and lung cancer. By defining the health risks of smoking and getting it in the public record, people clearly understood the cost, which inspired them to then change their behavior. This report laid the framework for a public education campaign that has continued ever since, which has greatly contributed to a reduction in the percentage of Americans who smoke.

When I speak to company representatives, it is rare that I find anyone who can tell me the cost of turnover per position, or the cost of turnover to the entire organization. They understand it is high, but they haven't actually quantified it, so they tend to take it less seriously. The *Turnover Calculator* acts like a Surgeon General's report; it opens the organization's eyes to turnover's true impact, specific to their company. This has the power of motivating them to do something about it.

YOUR MOST APPRECIABLE AND VALUABLE ASSET

In the mid 1980s, my husband took a job at Rocky Mountain Sports in Atlanta, Georgia. It is an award-winning retail store that has been Atlanta's local ski and snowboard shop since 1973. He was hired to be one of six guys whose responsibilities were to work the sales floor and tune-up skis and mount bindings. Jim says it was such a cool place to work! Two of the salesmen, along with Jim, were new to the team and not real avid skiers. Two more of the salesmen had been with the store for a few seasons and were better skiers. And then there was Gary. Gary was the man! He had been with the store for a long time and was the owner's right-hand man. A very good skier, his knowledge of the equipment was excellent. He was familiar with the great ski resorts all over the country and could tell people all about them. Customers would come to the store all the time and ask for Gary because he had taken good care of them in the past or they were told to go in and ask for Gary. His sales numbers were always the best by far! He trained all the new guys how to tune-up skis and mount bindings. With all his experience, his value to the store was tremendous!

Your employees are appreciable assets. The longer they are with the organization the more knowledgeable they become about systems, processes, products, clients, and the entire business. Their value to the company grows because they are equipped to add more and more value. One case study from Maia Josebachvili, VP of People at Greenhouse, found that keeping one salesperson for three years instead of two produced "a difference of 1.3 million dollars in net value to the company over a three year period." This study clearly reveals that the name of the game is to hold on to your valuable employees for as long as you can.

Of course, not every employee is an asset that grows in value. There are employees who stagnate, who never grow, who lack the ambition to take it to the next level. They are content to just get by. We would probably prefer that these employees just move on if they cannot or will not change.

The *Retention Architecture* is there to retain the valuable employees who continue to appreciate in value, and to turn the less productive employees into ones who can add value to the organization.

FOR FURTHER REFLECTION

As we move into Part II: *Retention Architecture*, consider your turnover rate and the hard and soft costs associated with employees deciding to leave. Now knowing the average cost of losing an employee, consider how your profit would increase by shifting your employees' dominant mindset forward.

1. What member of your team would be especially hard to lose?

2. What are some of the intangible costs you or your team experience when employees leave the organization?

3. Is your company retention rate in line with your industry average?

4. What cost surprised you the most in the *Turnover Calculator*?

5. How much time do you spend finding, hiring, and training new employees? If that time could be cut in half, what could you do with that time?

Part II

Retention Architecture

RETENTION ARCHITECTURE

Talent Acquisition

Trusted Leadership

Conflict Management

Talent Development

HR Practices

ColeneROGERS
THE TALENT KEEPER

Talent Acquisition

M y in-laws recently moved into a senior living community. It is the perfect solution for them, now that they are both over eighty years old. The building is brand new, so it is fresh and bright, with beautifully designed and decorated community spaces along with comfortable apartments for the residents. We joke that they live on a luxury cruise ship.

The website for this senior housing community is well designed, with a very clean look and just the right amount of text for effective messaging. There are gorgeous pictures that make you want to live there. On the website the company boasts of "exceptional services, superior dining options, dynamic engagement opportunities, luxurious amenities, and robust wellness programs, making it the ideal destination to enhance your vibrant way of life." Wow! That's a lot to live up to.

In making these statements, the owners and executives of this community are doing what most businesses do, they are putting their very best foot forward in the promises they make to customers and clients. Companies will often express the ideal image they have of themselves through their mission and marketing statements. It is what they imagined they would be when they first thought of starting the business. This is what I call their *Business Image Ideal*. It represents the very best they have to offer. And it makes sense that companies do this. They exist in very competitive markets where they need to appeal to enough customers to make a profit.

But those promises are only as good as the people who are entrusted to keep them, the employees. Jim's parents can live in the most beautiful building in all of Tallahassee with the best amenities, but without a good cook and an engaged wait staff, without a warm and friendly person at the front door where guests check in, without an administrator who diligently responds to all the residents' needs and requests, they will fail to be "exceptional," as their website claims. And the reality is most businesses, to some degree, fall short of their *Business Image Ideal*. I call this their *Business Image Shortfall*.

You've heard the saying, "If you want something done right, do it yourself." But doing it yourself is not possible or scalable in most businesses. To bring their vision to the marketplace, a business owner will have to delegate the responsibilities to employees. Having the infrastructure in place is not enough, you have to have the right people to run it.

INTERVIEWING TO REVEAL EMOTIONAL INTELLIGENCE AND MINDSET

So what do you look for in these employees whom you have to depend on to make your business a success? When considering who to hire, the smartest companies pay strong attention to the personality traits of the applicants because these identify those who are most likely to have future success. No matter the age or sex or type of work, there are common traits that the best employees exhibit.

- Dependable: Employees you can count on to show up on time, be prepared, and get the job done.
- Passionate: Employees who are passionate about life and the opportunities life presents are by nature engaged and productive.
- Amiable: Employees who like people and are friendly, sociable, and agreeable are a positive influence within the organization, bringing people together.
- Honest: Honest employees have integrity and can be trusted with what matters most to the organization.
- Team player: Team players work well with others. They understand there is strength in numbers and the biggest achievements and best ideas are usually the result of people working together.
- Confident: A confident person is usually confident for good reason. They possess self-belief they gained through experience. Confident people are natural leaders, which every company needs.
- Humble: Humble employees don't try to take all the credit, and they are willing to admit their mistakes. This provides a great example to others in the organization. They would rather let their actions do the talking than their words.
- Ambitious: Employees who are upward and forward thinking naturally seek and fill leadership positions within organizations. You

can count on them to think outside the box and generate new ideas and approaches.

• Integrity: Employees with integrity can be trusted to do the right thing, even at their own expense. Sometimes it takes just one person to speak up to prevent the whole company from doing the wrong thing.

• Communication skills: The work of any organization is carried out through hundreds of conversations taking place every day. Good communicators get business done efficiently and with fewer mistakes. These people can represent the organization well when interacting with customers and clients.

• Initiative: Employees with initiative don't have to be told what to do next. When they see an opportunity to improve a process, they act. These action-oriented people make things happen.

• Organized: Success rarely travels without organization. Organized employees finish projects on time and within budget. Organized employees give customers and clients confidence in the organization.

• Flexible: Flexible employees understand that events don't always happen as planned. They are ready and willing to go the extra mile to fulfill a task. Flexible people are not complainers.

• Enthusiastic: Enthusiasm is contagious and employees who express it are a wonderful influence within the organization. Enthusiasm keeps the positive energy flowing which keeps teams engaged and productive.

The traits listed above are often put into the category of what is called emotional intelligence. The emotional intelligence of an applicant will not be revealed in their resume, so questions need to be asked in the interview to draw these out. For example, would you describe yourself as a person who takes initiative? What does taking initiative look like to you? Can you name a time when you took the initiative? Were you comfortable taking initiative? When you have exhausted this line of questioning, you will have a picture of the initiative level of the applicant.

I've conducted countless interviews, and it is a skill that improves over time with practice. The goal is to identify qualified candidates who are a good fit for your organization who will stay with you. Keep in mind that candidates come to you with a certain mindset about your organization. They see you as *Insignificant*, *Temporary*, *Exclusive*, or as a *Career Company*. Just as questions can be asked to reveal emotional intelligence, questions can be asked to reveal the mindset of the applicant. If you can discover their mindset, you can make a more informed decision about offering them a job.

Jim attended the University of Indiana and graduated with a bachelor's degree in marketing. During his sophomore year, he met Carl, a keyboard player, singer and songwriter. Jim played guitar, and soon the two were writing songs together and making plans to form a band and pursue a music career after they both graduated. Jim finished school a year and a half before Carl, so while he waited for Carl to graduate, he worked jobs that were never intended to be a career.

During this time Jim's dad encouraged him to pursue a job with a company called Ryerson Steel. His dad worked for FMC, which did business with Ryerson, and he was told by a Ryerson salesman that they were hiring for inside sales positions. Jim reminded his dad of his plans to pursue music once Carl graduated, but his dad convinced him to interview for the job anyway. Going into the interview, Jim had an *Insignificant* mindset about Ryerson Steele. His plan was to give it a try, but he really didn't think music and steel would mix. Through their interview questioning, the company did not draw this mindset out, and they made Jim an offer. It was a decision he struggled with, but in the end, he said yes. Eleven months later, Jim resigned from his job to pursue a music career. And with that they lost all the money they had invested in Jim.

FINDING CANDIDATES

While working with companies to help them strengthen their *Retention Architecture*, I typically begin with an organizational audit. I want to see what systems they have in place to acquire talent, develop leaders, manage talent, resolve conflict, and stay in compliance with government regulations. One of the areas I focus on is their talent acquisition process, searching to discover if they have a talent acquisition strategy. I want to see everything they do to attract, find, and hire new employees. I look at their website, the job sites they use to post job openings, their application process, their handling of employee referrals, and more. Setting up a talent acquisition program is a big project, but it is well worth your time.

In one such audit I performed, the company was making the application process for its truck drivers and field workers too difficult. The job candidate had to print the application from the website, fill it out, scan it, and then email it back to the company. This is something most applicants will know how to do, but they may not own their own scanner, or they may be short on time, or whatever. It can be just enough of an inconvenience to make them say forget it. I told the person in charge of the process that they have to make it as easy and convenient as possible because that is what candidates want. The obvious answer is to have an online application potential employees fill out and send to the employer, all within the company website.

Here are some ideas to bring into your talent acquisition program:

- Good candidates have multiple offers. Companies that interview a good candidate should be ready to make an offer or risk losing them to a competing offer. If the hiring process takes too long, candidates start paying attention to other opportunities. You have to be faster than your competition.
- Consider hiring less qualified candidates who could get up to speed quickly with training.
- Build into your daily or weekly schedule talent acquisition activities and networking. Reach out to potential candidates and build relationships with people you can keep in a future employee file.
- Consider candidates from different walks of life such as people looking to change industries, stay-at-home moms reentering the workforce, consultants and small business owners.

- Trade out experienced candidates for candidates with a specific skill set.
- Offer more flexible work schedules.
- Project three-to-six months ahead for when you need to fill leadership and specialty positions. This helps you be ready with potential candidates when the time comes.
- Think of your talent acquisition as a sales process. Get the whole company involved.
- Partner with universities and job fairs.

FINDING EMPLOYEES IN NEW PLACES

Companies with an Insignificant or Temporary dominant mindset often struggle to find qualified candidates to fill open positions. When there is a shortage of labor due to a strong economy, even the best companies are challenged to find candidates. It becomes necessary then to go and find employees in places where you haven't looked before. One of my clients, U.S. Submergent Technologies (USST) based in Orlando, Florida, did just that.

With their patented one-of-a-kind technology, USST removes sand, grit, and other residuals from underwater areas or other liquid environments, including structures such as tanks and pipes. The work of a field technician is hard and demanding, and it can be difficult to find guys to do that work, especially in a tight labor market.

Without setting out to hire the previously incarcerated, they had a favorable experience with an employee named Paul who had served time in jail. Paul displayed such a strong work ethic and company loyalty, born out of his gratitude for getting a second chance in life, that USST wanted to find more guys like him. Gretchen Peterson, CHRO of Dave's Killer Bread Foundation, a non-profit foundation dedicated to inspiring and equipping employers to embrace Second Chance Employment describes in this way what guys like Paul demonstrate. "Our formerly incarcerated aren't just 'nonproblems.' They're role models in terms of performance, attendance and teamwork. They have an especially strong incentive to deliver value because they've seen the alternative, and, in the overwhelming majority of cases, they deliver."

Paul introduced USST to Jobs Partnership, a faith-based organization in Orlando, Florida, that works with the previously incarcerated to help them transition back into society by finding and placing them in jobs with a future. Jobs Partnership provides a twelve-week class where attendees learn leadership skills through the use of biblical stories along with what it means to be a good employee. They also learn practical skills like preparing a resume, interviewing, and doing basic personal finance.

Hiring the previously incarcerated has proved to be a successful initiative for U.S. Submergent Technologies. Paul is now an operational manager and two other employees that were hired through Jobs Partnership are supervisors.

ONBOARDING

In the places where I've worked as a recruiter, I would develop a kind of motherly relationship with those employees I recruited into the company. I brought them into our world by selling them on the idea of working for us, so I felt responsible for how they were getting along and being treated.

I recruited at a high-level state agency in Florida

where there was no real onboarding process to speak of, which made it hard on "momma recruiter." Each of the managers did their own thing to get their employees plugged in and situated, and as you would expect, some were better at it than others. I was always a little anxious on the new employee's first day.

One such employee was hired to fill an entry level position in the accounting department. After he filled out his paperwork, someone from his department came to escort him to the floor on which he would be working, and I wished him well. A couple days later, I took the elevator up to check on how he was doing, and what I found left me embarrassed for the agency and feeling bad for him. He did not yet have a desk or computer or phone. When I inquired about this with his manager, he showed me a closet they were clearing out to make room for his desk. The new employee was gone within thirty days, deciding he wanted to work somewhere else.

Different ideas exist about when onboarding begins, what it entails, and how long it should last. Is it accomplished in one day, one week, or one year? Is it just giving the new employee their desk and making introductions…or is it more than that?

You will recall that I identified two stages an employee goes through within the *Employee Engagement Environment*, the *Integration* stage and the *Ownership* stage. Onboarding begins when the employee first enters the *Integration* stage, when they first make contact with the company, before they are hired, and includes everything the company does after that, within the *Integration* stage, to attract, hire, and make the employee a productive member of the organization.

Researchers have uncovered a clear correlation

between onboarding and three other things, engagement, productivity, and retention. This makes one shake their head, wondering why so many organizations fail to implement an effective onboarding program. Here are just some studies and statistics.

- Eighty-eight percent of employees think their employer did a poor job with the onboarding process. (Gallup, 2017)
- A 2009 study by the Aberdeen Group of senior executives and HR staffing and recruiting functions found that 86 percent of respondents felt that a new hire's decision to stay with a company long-term is made within the first six months of employment.
- A 2007 study from the Wynhurst Group found that newly hired employees are 58 percent more likely to still be at the company three years later if they had completed a structured onboarding process.
- The Aberdeen Group reported that 66 percent of companies with onboarding programs claimed a higher rate of successful assimilation of new hires into company culture, 62 percent had higher time-to-productivity ratios, and 54 percent reported higher employee engagement.
- Statistics compiled by Click Boarding, an onboarding software company in Eden Prairie, Minnesota, show the value of a structured onboarding process or program: New employees who went through a structured onboarding program were 58 percent more likely to be with the organization after three years.

I mentioned earlier that the state agency I recruited for lacked an onboarding program. As an employee, I too had my first day of work at the agency, and there was definitely no red carpet or welcome sign. I was hired with the understanding that I would be groomed to take over as manager of the HR department when the present manager retired. So I was somewhat humbled when I received my desk, which was positioned right near to the door of our department. I felt more like a receptionist than a future manager in training. There was no lunch planned to formally introduce me to my team members, so I went home to grab a quick bite. My husband was there and being surprised to see me, he asked how my morning went. I wasn't ready to share my true feelings, in truth I was still processing it all, so I said it went pretty well. But inside I was thinking, *What have I done?* Looking back now I see that on that first day, the seeds were planted for my eventual departure. I left one-and-a-half years later for another opportunity.

FOR FURTHER REFLECTION

We've taken a look at promises made to customers that reveal a *Business Image Ideal* and potentially, a *Business Image Shortfall*. Here are a few considerations for you to think about before we dive into leadership in the next chapter.

1. What are the promises your company makes to clients and customers as expressed in your *Business Image Ideal*?

2. Does your organization do a good job of hiring employees to minimize your *Business Image Shortfall*?

3. Where has your organization found success in finding talent?

4. What new talent acquisition solutions are you willing to try?

5. Describe the onboarding process you experienced when you joined the organization. Has it changed since then?

Chapter 5

Leadership: The Foundation of Retention Architecture

Leadership supports and informs every initiative in the *Retention Architecture*. All your efforts to attract and acquire qualified employees, develop meaningful relationships with your employees, resolve conflict in a timely manner, have open and honest conversations with your employees about their future with the company, and all HR best practices will crumble if leadership is not there to provide support.

Leadership informs every retention initiative in an effort to help relieve you of the frustrations of high turnover by:

- Improving the *Integration* stage of the *Employee Life Cycle* so employees find a place to fit in and belong in the organization.
- Encouraging the employees who take initiative in the *Ownership* stage.
- Increasing the engagement level of employees in the *Employee Engagement Environment*.

MARK: A STORY OF LEADERSHIP

My husband and I live on a golf course, or at least we used to. It was a twenty-seven-hole course made up of the North nine, the South nine, and the East nine. Our house is located on what was the fourth hole of the North that the owner closed, saying he wanted to devote all resources to improving and maintaining the South and the East. It eventually surfaced that the owner's true intention was to repurpose the land of the North for single and multi-dwelling homes.

Back in the early 1980s he had marketed the land as a golf course community and people bought homes based on the belief that they would always live on a golf course. Therefore, the resident homeowners believed he was violating the original contract with his plans to build, so a lawsuit was filed to prevent him from doing so. If the owner won the suit, all of our property values were sure to go down.

While the case moved through the courts, almost all maintenance on the North came to a stop. The golf club, still maintaining the other eighteen holes, committed to mowing the North just four times a year. The change was striking and sad! Our once beautifully manicured fourth hole had turned into field filled with fire ants and every weed known to man.

One Saturday afternoon, when the Florida sun was at its highest, I saw a man with a large brimmed sun hat, riding on a John Deere cutting the field. It was Mark, a neighbor we knew from his annual fireworks display on New Year's Eve. I watched him cut for three hours that day, and again the next day, until the entire hole was mowed. The next time Mark cut, I saw that he had recruited another neighbor, Tim, to cut with him on his smaller riding mower. And then Margaret joined the cutting squad with her John Deere. The consistent mowing was beginning to make a difference, it was starting to look like a version of its old self.

But Mark wasn't satisfied. There was more he wanted to do, so he went around to all the residents and invited everyone to a meeting of the Friends of the Fourth Hole. One late afternoon, about fifteen of us gathered in lawn chairs near where the green once was and listened to what Mark had to say. First, he updated us on the progress of the court case against the owner. Being a lawyer and a part of the legal team representing the residents in the case against the owner of the golf course, Mark knew all the details. He informed us how the legal team was doing everything they could to protect our property values. He then patiently answered all of our questions.

Next he talked about the upkeep of the fourth hole. He shared his plans to purchase a commercial mower and continue to cut, then fertilize, and finally treat for insects. He came organized and prepared with a handout showing previous and future costs. Once again, he took our questions and then asked for our creative input on the whole project. Finally, he asked everyone to contribute a fixed amount of money, if they could, to help cover all the costs along with our commitment to chip in on the work. By the end of the meeting, everyone had caught Mark's vision. They signed up to help with the work and people wrote checks to help cover the cost.

Because of Mark's leadership, we could once again look out our back window and see a beautiful green space.

LEADERSHIP IS INFLUENCE

Leadership is a big word to get your arms around. It's like trying to wrap your arms around a redwood tree. Volumes of books have been written on the topic. John Maxwell, who tops the list of leadership gurus, has written over seventy books, most of them on the topic of leadership. Obviously, there is a lot to say about leadership. So to distill the definition of leadership down to a single sentence is not easy; it might not even be possible. As a certified John Maxwell trainer, I am very familiar with John's definition, and it is as good as anything else I've heard. Thus we will use his definition going forward. John says leadership is influence, nothing more and nothing less. It is not about the position, office, or title. Because if you can't influence people to follow you then you are not leading them anywhere. Margaret Thatcher said, "Being in power is like being a lady. If you have to tell people you are then you are not."

The story of Mark gives us a picture of leadership. Here are a few things Mark showed us:

- Leaders don't need a title.
- Leaders lead by example.
- Leaders see possibility and opportunity where others do not.
- Leaders recruit others to have more impact.
- Leaders are relational.
- Leaders get things done.

LEADERSHIP IS JUST PART OF THE GIG

Because we all have people we influence, we are all leaders. Some of us have more, some of us have less, but no one lives without influencing someone. When Jim started a business teaching students how to play the guitar, it was a way to earn income by doing something he enjoyed. He didn't think of it as a position of leadership, he saw himself as a teacher. But teachers wield influence, so Jim is definitely a leader to his students. At Jim's guitar recitals, parents often tell me that, besides Jim being a great guitar instructor, he is a great mentor and leader to their son or daughter. Some have added they would pay twice as much for lessons just to have his influence.

So being a leader isn't necessarily a conscious choice that automatically comes with an office or title to go with the position. A lot of times leadership is just part of the gig. If you are a husband, father, mother, or single parent, you are a leader in your home. If you are the best player on your football or softball team, the other players look up to you, which gives you influence, which makes you a leader.

LEADERSHIP THAT COMES WITH A TITLE

Then there are the leadership opportunities we choose to pursue or that are offered to us that come with a title attached. I chose to accept the offer to be vice president of the Big Bend Society of Human Resources in the state of Florida. In reality, I was offered the position of president because the standard practice was for the vice president to automatically become president once the acting president's term was complete. This is how we are accustomed to recognize and respond to leadership, as a position with a title.

LEADERS MAKE AN ORGANIZATION BETTER OR WORSE

The Florida State University (FSU) is located in Tallahassee, Florida. A resident of Tallahassee since 1999, I use to follow the Seminoles football program only out of the corner of my eye. I loved Bobby Bowden and was aware of all his success there, but I really didn't watch. Then Jimbo Fisher took over and reenergized the program, bringing home a national championship in 2013. But at that time, I was watching Auburn, where my oldest son was enrolled, so I still wasn't really watching FSU.

All of that changed when my son left Auburn and transferred to Florida State. Now I was watching! I saw their success diminish as Jimbo started to check out, going 7–6 in his final season. Jimbo left for Texas A&M, leaving the Seminoles in a weakened state. The Seminoles then hired Willie Taggert, a coach with an overall winning percentage of .500 in his combined time at Western Kentucky, South Florida, and Oregon. You knew it wasn't going well when the fans of FSU's in-state rival, the Miami Hurricanes, wore t-shirts that read, Hey FSU, Keep Willie! Willie went 9–12 over one and a half seasons and was fired halfway through the 2019–2020 season.

FSU football is now in the hands of coach Mike Norvell who arrived by way of Memphis, enjoying good success there as the Tiger's head coach. As with any organization, the Florida State football program will get better or worse based on the quality of coach

Norvell's leadership, just as it did with Jimbo Fisher and Willie Taggert. All the best coach Mike, I'll be watching!

WILL YOU MAKE THINGS BETTER OR WORSE?

The choice each one of us has to make is will we lead well. Will we be a force for good? Will we make things better, or will we make things worse?

To frame our discussion going forward, I do need to make a distinction. Leadership in the hands of the wrong person is never good, and it can be dangerous. Much of world history is the story of tyrants and the death and destruction they unleashed. There is a proverb that John Maxwell has made popular but did not create, and I often repeat it from the leadership platform, "He that thinketh he leadeth and hath no one following him is only taking a walk." Someone might try and make the argument that Hitler was a great leader, he certainly had his share of followers and he was able to influence a lot of people to do what he wanted, but measuring the magnitude of the results or the degree of influence is not our only criteria. Leadership should be judged by the standard of doing what is right for the betterment of others within the bounds of the law and common decency.

The story of leadership is filled with the successes and failures of well-known leaders from all walks of life, from every field and occupation. Your life may not be as high profile as a Mark Zuckerburg or Donald Trump, but the consequences of your leadership in your life is no less. We know you have influence, the question for you is what will you do with it?

LEADERS ARE NOT BORN, THEY ARE MADE

Are there born leaders? If you are asking if people are born with all of the traits necessary to be a good leader, the answer is no. There are many qualities that come together to make a good leader, but let's look at the leader's character to make the point that leaders were not born ready to lead.

The virtues of humility, compassion, empathy, honesty, and sincerity are never fully formed in an infant or young child. The conditions might be present for those virtues to blossom but there is no guarantee they will take root. A life is made up of a million decisions that will determine the character of a person. A baby crying because they are hungry is not a decision. You are not born with character. Character is formed in the crucible of life, one decision at a time.

If leaders are not born leaders, then they are made. But made by what? How are they made?

LEADERS ARE MADE BY THEIR CHOICES

At the age of seven I sang my first solo in front of an audience. I was in a Christmas production called Little Blue Angel, and I remember standing on that stage thinking, *I really like this!* Wanting to feel that way again, my parents helped me find more opportunities to act and sing throughout my teenage years.

When I reached early adulthood, I became very involved in regional musical theater in Central Florida where I had lived my whole life. I acted and sang in musicals throughout my 20s and halfway through my 30s. I entered into the musical theater scene with lots of experience that helped me earn the lead role in most every musical I was in. I was Mabel in *Pirates of Penzance*, Eliza Doolittle in *My Fair Lady*, Magnolia in *Showboat*, I was the lead in *Carousel*, the *Sound of Music*, *Fantastics*, *1776,* and many more.

At a church I was attending in Orlando, the leadership wanted to put on a simple play and, knowing I was an actress, they asked if I would direct. I guess I figured I had taken so much onstage direction that it was my turn to give some, so I said yes.

At one of our performances, I remember this gentleman walked in to watch and I thought to myself, well he thinks a lot of himself, but I quickly forgot he was there. It wasn't long afterward, though, that he reentered the scene by giving me a phone call. He said his name was Dan Holland, and he was the pastor of a nearby church named Metro Church. He shared that he had recently visited a very influential church in Chicago where they used drama to help minister to their congregation. He liked it so much that he wanted to bring drama to his church. He must have liked our little play, either that or he didn't have anyone else to ask, but either way he offered me a part-time position as drama director at Metro Church. I accepted and spent three wonderful years there! By the way, Dan became a dear friend, and I learned that what I saw that first day was nothing close to arrogance but a humble confidence.

From there I found myself in Tallahassee where I joined a church that just happened to also have a drama ministry. Though I didn't actively pursue the director's chair, it somehow found me. I spent ten years there as the drama director where we built elaborate sets for Broadway-length shows that ran over several nights.

Leaders are made through the choices they make

while they naturally live their lives. The choices we make are often a response to the activities we enjoy or are good at. I think the advice we've all heard to follow your heart is good. Your heart can take you places you never thought possible. In my story, at the age of seven, finding myself at home on a stage and loving it, proved to be the realization that propelled me to sing and act, which ultimately led me to lead a ministry with over a hundred volunteers.

LEADERS HAVE A YES MINDSET

Jim was asked by the leader of the high school seniors at our church if he would spend an hour with the class and share his story of faith (along with anything else he desired to share) to encourage the students. He had to think for a second before responding because he didn't have an hour talk prepared and sitting in his drawer, so agreeing to share with the students meant he would have to spend some time in preparation. And besides that, he had very little public speaking experience, which meant the talk would be a little nerve racking. It didn't matter, he said yes because what could be gained was far greater than any cost.

Life will present you with countless opportunities to expand your influence, but increased influence requires you to step out of your comfort zone and say yes. Do you know someone whose natural inclination is to say no to new experiences? You might even recognize some of that in yourself. Putting on a yes mindset will prevent no from limiting your life experiences and your influence. I call this living a lifestyle of yes. Be ready to say yes when opportunity presents itself. By saying yes to Dan Holland's job offer, a whole new world opened for me, filled with rich relationships and rewards. You never know where yes will take you.

"NO" IS THE MARK OF A TRUE LEADER

Matthew Henry, in his Bible commentary, said that it is a very dangerous thing for a man to act against his conscience, even if it is mistaken. One of the most important actions a leader can take is saying no when the world around him is saying yes. That is why leaders get paid the big bucks, to keep the car out of the ditch, to see the trouble ahead, to say to his squad I know it looks good right now, but this won't end well. Choosing to say no when everyone else is saying yes is the true mark of a leader. It might be lonely at first, but in time the truth will keep you company.

LEADERSHIP IS A LEARNABLE SKILL

There are degrees and certifications that people can earn in leadership, but most people learn to lead without them. Leadership is a learnable skill, but for many it is a skill left unstudied or ignored. Some people are so busy leading that they don't have time to even think about the study of leadership.

One of the first skills that Jim teaches his guitar students is the ability to make simple chord changes. The aspiring guitarist will repeatedly change between the most popular chords, and simply by practicing it over and over again they will eventually learn to change chords quickly, which is what is needed to play songs. With the right technique, the task is accomplished sooner and in a way that sets them up for future success.

But Jim has observed that people who learn on their own, without ever seeking outside guidance, can develop bad habits of hand position that hurt their progress in the long run. Having found a way on their own, they are resistant to fix the poor technique because that would mean relearning what they already have learned.

In a similar way, leaders can and will find their own answers and way of doing things. But their solution, even though it is getting the job done now, could end up hurting them in the long run. I coach leaders to take full advantage of the wealth of leadership material available to them. It is far better to learn from others' mistakes than from our own. Left to our own devices it can take much longer to learn a leadership principle when it was available the whole time for us to learn.

IS IN THE APPLICATION

You can study the principles of effective leadership, but until you put them into practice, they will live as somewhat lifeless principles on the page. It is so exciting to put newly acquired leadership skills on the field and watch them score points for your team.

FOR FURTHER REFLECTION

After considering leadership defined as influence and the various ways we lead, either with or without a title, by our actions, and so on, consider the following questions that relate to your own leadership of others.

1. Think of someone in your life who was or is a great leader. What qualities do you see in them that are worth emulating?

2. Identify all the areas in your life where you have measurable influence.

3.   Would you describe yourself as having a "yes mindset" as defined in this book?

4.   Can you think of a time when you said no as a leader when others wanted to say yes?

5.   This book defines leadership as influence. How would you define leadership?

Chapter 6

Self-Leadership

I am not of much value to my fellow man if I'm not much value to myself. If my own house is not in order, how can I help others get their house in order? If I can't lead myself, then how can I hope to lead others?

John Maxwell was the first person I heard speak about leading yourself. He said, "Learning to lead yourself well is one of the most important things you'll ever do as a leader." Leading oneself can be a strange concept to get your mind around. Don't you need at least one other person if you're going to lead? There is a Bible verse that sheds some light on the idea. "That man should not think that he will receive anything from the Lord, he is a double minded man, unstable in all he does" (James 1:7). That verse speaks of a man being of two minds. Put that way, I can begin to understand and relate to the idea of leading yourself.

Within us all are two minds competing, the mind of what I ought to do and the mind of what I want to do. The more the two agree, the less divided we are. Now I'm pretty sure my two minds will never agree on German chocolate cake frosting. I will always want to eat more frosting than I ought to. But our wants never live in isolation from our other wants. I also want to be able to fit into the clothes that are in my closet right now, which competes with my want to eat German chocolate frosting. On top of that, both have to answer to what I know I ought to do which is take good care of myself. This explains why I lean over with my fork and only take a small bite from my husband's piece of cake.

To be clear, our wants compete against each other, and each and every want is guided to some degree by what we know we ought to do. This internal struggle is everyone's challenge, no person lives life without it. People who are described as having self-discipline make it look easier and have more success with it than others. This term, self-discipline, brings us back to what John Maxwell said about the importance of leading oneself. I call it Self-Leadership.

THE CONFLICT OF COMPETING WANTS

Because you are filled with so many competing wants, you will live with some degree of internal conflict. I call this the *conflict of competing wants*. The conflict comes with deciding what you want to do at any given moment on any given day.

Part of the joy of my work is that I have the privilege of doing many different things: I give keynote speeches; I do lunch and learns and boardroom presentations; I do one-on-one executive coaching; group supervisor training; communication workshops; and team building exercises. All of this has to be informed with original thought, so I'm constantly mining for content, reflecting on what I read or heard, and then writing my own material. And finally, it all needs the support of marketing. Whew! So within the business there exists many competing wants. What can happen is that I begin working in one area and immediately think I should be working in another. This is a huge distraction that limits my progress until I am able to shake it off. When you add in my personal life, which is no less busy than my business life, I can experience a clash of competing wants.

YOUR DREAMS WILL GUIDE YOU

If we are going to be of any value to ourselves or to others, if we are to be excellent at what we do, it is essential that we identify what we really want out of life. What are the things you want to accomplish that would be a source of huge regret if you didn't ever do? If you think of accomplishments as destinations, knowing where you are going and what you want to pick up along the way will help you know what to do today, to do right now. For that, we turn to your dreams.

In an upcoming chapter on developing others, you will read more about a book entitled *The Dream Manager,* by Matthew Kelly. I bring it up now because it provides a worksheet for readers to identify and specify their dreams within twelve different categories.

Jim and I each did the dream exercise, and I can tell you it is energizing and life giving. As a Christian, I believe God wants us to dream and dream big! Jim and I were setting goals, but we were not dreaming—there is a difference between the two. Dreams are made of different material than goals. Dreams are lighter and more ethereal. They float in from the mist of our imagination; they visit future generations and affect family trees. By defining them we pull them down to earth long enough to hop on and ride them to new lands.

As Jim and I dreamed, we were creating our lives, saying out loud to each other what we wanted to happen, where we wanted to go, describing what a day will look like in five years, in ten years, the difference we want to make, the needs of others we want to help meet.

THE 12 DREAM CATEGORIES
FROM THE DREAM MANAGER:

1. Physical

2. Emotional

3. Intellectual

4. Spiritual

5. Psychological

6. Material

7. Professional

8. Financial

9. Creative

10. Adventure

11. Legacy

12. Character

From the vantage point of our dreams, we can see clearly to set goals and prioritize the actions that will equip us with the skills and knowledge for the journey. This gives us the clarity to know what to do at any given moment, which diminishes or even eliminates altogether the conflict of our competing wants. Like an aerodynamically designed vehicle, we can travel further with less resistance and more efficiency.

DREAMS REQUIRE YOU
TO LEAVE YOUR COMFORT ZONE

When I first launched my business, I was sitting at my kitchen table with my new website designer and developer, and he asked why at this stage in my life I was choosing to leave the security of working for a company to start my own. I laughed, "'At this stage in my life,' what are you trying to say?" This was a risky question to ask the woman who would be writing him a check for the next twenty-four months.

The truth is that I had asked myself that question more than once along the way to building this business. In those times, I was thankful for my husband Jim who has more of a stomach for risk than I do. He would remind me that I was seeking to increase my influence; that I was never completely satisfied working for others; that I was being true to myself.

He was right. I think I always wanted to work for myself, to control my own destiny. For me, creating my own business was the means to do this and enjoy a greater level of success. But this required that I get out of my comfort zone and stare failure down. I had to take the risk for the possibility of something greater.

In less philosophical terms and with far fewer words, I answered our web developer and said, "It just felt right."

GOAL SETTING IS A POWERFUL TOOL

In 2005, a friend convinced me to join eHarmony, the online dating site. One morning soon after that I checked my email and eHarmony said I had a new match. I clicked and it was Jim.

During our first phone conversation I asked him the often-used interview question, "Where do you want to be in five years?" He wasn't sure. It wasn't that he lived without direction or commitment, he just believed that if he worked hard and stayed true to his beliefs and values then the adventure would play out as it should. In other words, he was admittedly not a goal setter. No offense to Jim and those of you like him but that is an approach I do not recommend.

Goal setting is a powerful tool that should be in every leader's toolbox and in anyone else's who wants to accomplish more. Just think about how much you get done when there is a deadline.

For the last year and a half Jim and I have been talking about writing the book you are reading right now. Talking was good at first because with each conversation we breathed a little more life into the project. And then I went and did it; I promised an event planner that if she hired me to give their keynote I would have my book finished and available at her event. That sealed the deal—I got the job. Oops! "Hey honey, I got the gig. Oh, and I said we would have our book ready."

As the delivery date for the book grew ever closer, we figured a ghostwriter was the answer because neither Jim or I had ever written a book, and it just looked like too heavy of a lift. But then we both went and did it, we signed with a publisher and promised we would write the book ourselves and deliver the first draft of the manuscript in four weeks.

The deadline forced our hand. We took the total number of words needed for the book, divided by the total number of days available to write, which gave us a daily word count to produce. This served as a goal within the larger goal that helped us track our progress. We got up earlier, stayed up later, entertained ourselves less, all to reach that daily word count. Sometimes we failed to reach our daily goal but that was okay, we just got up and went for it the next day.

You won't always have a deadline like the one we created for ourselves to force our action. That is why we set goals. Goal setting is the artificial creation of deadlines. If you treat goals as deadlines, they work the same. To give them teeth go public with your personal goals by sharing them with certain individuals in your life. This helps create accountability that is similar to a deadline. I also write them down on sticky notes and place them where I can see them often.

For his young guitar students who aren't practicing, Jim will start with a question, "Is this your idea to play guitar, or is this your parent's idea?" Because the guitar is such a popular instrument to play, most say it is their idea. Having reconnected them to their desire, Jim will ask them to commit to four practices for the upcoming week. He gives them the freedom to say yes or no which creates buy in because they now feel the plan they are creating is their own. Then they identify the best days and the best time of day for each practice and write it down. Jim has to manage this step very closely to make sure they pick times that set them up for success.

Finally, he has them commit by saying very clearly that they intend to follow through, sometimes asking them to sign their name. This creates the accountability. And when they return the next week, he asks them how they did, and in almost every case the student who was not practicing has practiced.

Here are seven things that goals accomplish:

- Goals force us to take positive action.
- Goals increase the amount we produce.
- Goal setters make more money.
- Goals force us to manage our time, eliminating the unnecessary.
- Goals test and reveal our level of commitment.
- Goals create better processes.
- Goals make our dreams a reality.

WHAT WE DO TODAY DETERMINES WHO WE BECOME TOMORROW

The Art of Improvement is a channel on YouTube. One of the channel's video episodes is titled "7 Crucial Lessons People Often Learn Too Late In Life." It is very good! One of the lessons is "our everyday habits form our future selves." It describes how what you do today is one more action toward who you will be tomorrow. After an action is replicated over the course of one week, you begin to scratch the surface of change; after replicating an action over one month, you begin to notice a slight difference; after that action is carried out over one or more years, the degree of change will be such that you may not even recognize yourself.

A STORY OF REAL CHANGE

In 2002, Jim was diagnosed with ulcerative colitis. His doctor did not suggest any lifestyle changes but prescribed a daily dosage of Asacol, a medication to prevent the symptoms. Most of the time he felt normal, but occasionally he experienced a flare of the symptoms. When this happened, he was instructed to take a larger dose of medications to quell the symptoms. He lived like this for seventeen years when, at the tail end of that time, the Asacol had lost its effectiveness, and he was living with almost constant symptoms.

I decided to ask my nutritionist if she thought she could help Jim. She made a startling claim: with a change in his diet she could get him off all medication without any symptoms. Jim was quite skeptical, but to his credit, he agreed to go all in for a year, and then evaluate the progress. He already ate pretty well but big changes had to be made. No more milk, cheese (or dairy of any sort); only gluten free or sprouted bread; only red potatoes; no pork, and no food or drink with sugar. I recall the day before Jim was to start the new diet. We sat at a sidewalk table in Thomasville, Georgia, and enjoyed a delicious breakfast together, Jim with his French toast and bacon covered in syrup. I don't exaggerate when I say he was a sad man, feeling like his life was never going to be the same.

The progress was almost non-existent in the first few months, but he stuck to his diet each day, and eventually, we started to see improvement. At the six-month mark Jim started to reduce the amount of medication he was taking because the diet was working. He also told me that the new diet really wasn't that bad, and that he was starting to believe it was possible to be symptom and medication free. Within one year that is just what happened! We couldn't believe it! It has been three years since the change, and he is a completely different person in this regard. He is even able to occasionally eat many of the old foods he had to let go of, like French toast and bacon with syrup.

TOOLS FOR THE JOURNEY

The first tool is self-awareness. I think all of us look back at some specific event or a period in our lives and, with some regret, ask ourselves "what was I thinking?" If enough time has passed, we forget, and we're fooled into believing we weren't thinking at all. But there is always a reason for anything and everything we've ever done. There was something we wanted that took precedence over every other want we had at the time.

All of this is really evidence that we have learned a few things, that we are wiser, more experienced, and more mature than we were in times past. It would be more of a concern to me if I didn't ever ask myself that question.

I figure if I can ask, *What was I thinking?*, about past events, might I ask myself that same question in the future about things I am doing now. To try and prevent that, I occasionally take a self-assessment and ask questions like:

- How well am I treating people?
- Do I have genuine relationships with the people I work with?
- Do people know I care about them?

- Will I regret doing something I am doing now or regret not doing something?
- How do people perceive me?

I could fill a page with more questions like the ones above. The idea here is to build self-awareness by asking yourself meaningful questions to make sure your actions are aligned with your values, and you are staying true to your dreams and the goals you have set.

Self-forgiveness is another necessary tool. Regrets are a distraction. They have the power to haunt us and slow us down. You wouldn't run a marathon with a thirty-pound backpack. Be kind and forgive yourself for the sake of the cause. The cause is the fulfillment of your dreams. A lot is at stake and there is work to be done today. Yesterday has passed, so leave it there. Correct what needs to be corrected and get on with it. Great leaders learn from their past mistakes, so they don't continue to repeat them.

Keep an attitude of wonder. When I worked a nine-to-five job, I was around people all day. Now as an entrepreneur, my workday is filled with high concentrations of people in short bursts, followed by time spent alone preparing for the next burst. Thank goodness I have Bubby, my son's cat, to keep me company.

Bubby is funny, he does what I am about to describe literally every time. When I click print on my laptop and the printer wakes up, no distance is too far for him to come running for the show. He jumps up on the desk and looks with wonder and curiosity in the space where the paper is being pushed out. When the printer goes back to sleep, Bubby is still there staring in.

How does he do it? How does he come to the printer

with such a fresh attitude every time? It is quite an admirable trait really. I wouldn't want the printer to have that effect on me, but I'd like my job to always have that effect on me. I'd like the people and the opportunities and everything that everyday has to offer to fill me with wonder and excitement as if it was all happening for the first time.

I've watched YouTube videos that show adults actually hearing sound for the first time after receiving a cochlear implant. Loved ones are with them and there are tears of joy as the person experiences the wonder of sound for the first time. I know it isn't possible or natural for those people to sustain that level of amazement, because the reality is that the amazing becomes ordinary. But Bubby reminds me that this is an amazing world we live in! A world I want to run to with an attitude of wonder and excitement!

Have an attitude to remember why. Jim has a guitar teaching studio here in Tallahassee. When he first established it after moving from Atlanta in 2006, it was all about getting new students. Each new student he acquired was cause for a mini celebration because he was building the business. He has since enjoyed a full schedule for many years, but he says that on the rare day when it all feels a little mundane, and he hears the footsteps of his next student walking up the steps, he reminds himself how exciting it was in the beginning when students walked in. The memory only takes a second to flip the switch on Jim's perspective, and he is ready to give each and every student his very best.

We can forget why we went into business in the first place, and how excited we were, or the thrill we felt saying, "I got the job!" Remember why and boost your attitude.

Keep your self-talk positive. Have you noticed that all the best things exist at higher altitudes and we have to climb to reach them? A positive frame of mind is one of those things. Our natural state is more pessimistic than optimistic. To be optimistic and positive means we have to make a conscious effort to be so. That said, we are creatures of conversation, and the person we talk to the most is ourselves. This self-talk is really just our thoughts about anything and everything. Just like we want to manage and edit what we say to others, it is important we do the same for ourselves because it affects how everything shows up to us.

You have a say in what you say to yourself; you have a say in how the world shows up to you; you have a say in how you see your company, your future there, and the people you work with.

It matters because you will need everything working in your favor to succeed.

FOR FURTHER REFLECTION

This chapter is packed with self-leadership tools and information. So how is your self-leadership going? Think about the following questions carefully. Take the time to really consider where you are in life now, consider your conflicting wants and how you're managing those, your dreams, goals, dreams, plans...

1. How do you manage the *conflict of competing wants* in your personal and professional life to prioritize what needs to be done?

2. What is that one big item that has been on your to do list for far too long?

3. Define and fill out your dream for one category from the 12 categories of dreams.

4. Has setting goals served you in your life as a leader? Describe.

5. Identify one action you could take repeatedly over time that would make a powerful difference in your life.

Chapter 7

Trust and Character

Winston Churchill was not a fan of exercise but that didn't prevent him from walking miles at a time, among the smoke and rubble of bombed buildings, to comfort the people of London in a show of solidarity.

It was World War II and the Battle of Britain was being fought in the skies above the besieged nation. The Germans began by targeting shipping and harbor facilities in northern and southern England, and then they made a deadly shift in strategy, targeting civilian populations in London. The repetitive raids ultimately killed more than forty-three thousand people and wounded twice the amount.

When the London blitz started, there was no holding Winston back. Against the wishes of his cabinet ministers, he would take to the streets, despite the dangers, to be with the suffering citizens of London.

To keep Winston from taking the most dangerous routes, his wife, Clementine, insisted on going with him. Day after day they walked through the streets of London, listening to the needs of the now homeless. Because of this he was idolized by the people. And they knew they could trust Winston with all the power and authority of a nation to execute the war because he would not use it like a tyrant.

TRUST: THE FOUNDATION OF RELATIONSHIPS

The more power someone has the more we hope we can trust them because the more power they have, the more damage they can do. This is why who we elect as president of our country is so very important. But trust doesn't just pertain to matters of state, it is involved in virtually every human transaction. Parents trust their teenagers with the car, parents trust the babysitter with their kids, friends trust friends with their secrets, employers trust their employees with an expensive piece of equipment. Before a woman allows herself to fall in love with a man, she would be wise to ask herself, *Can I trust this guy with my heart?* (or vice versa).

Trust is the foundation for so many of the relationships you and I have in our lives. The degree to which trust is involved is indicative of the kind of relationship we have with that person and how much we've entrusted them with. Trust is paramount in my relationship with Jim. If either one of us breaks that trust both our lives will forever change. On the other hand, when we are taking a walk, Jim and I will say hello to our neighbor Tim who is typically playing fetch with his dog. Tim is a such a nice man! We will have short but meaningful conversations and then we'll say, "have a great evening!" Trust is not much of a factor in our relationship with Tim because there is nothing we've entrusted him with or vice versa. If we were to ever confide in Tim trust would become more of a factor.

TRUST IS DOING WHAT YOU SAY

It is competitive out there! To get hired for any speaking gig, I have to go up against hundreds of speakers. So to be chosen to give a keynote, I need everything working in my favor, one of the most important being my website and my overall online presence. The website must have the right messaging and the right design to engage the viewer and to increase screen time and per-page visits. It must be optimized for viewing on all the devices, computer, iPad, and phone. And it needs to communicate with our CRM (customer relationship management software) to capture emails, so I can nurture relationships.

The first generation of my website looked great, but it lacked functionality. It was the source of a lot of frustration, the kind only technology can bring. So I hired a web developer who said he could be my savior and make all my technological sins go away. Using a few words we had never heard before, he described how he would rebuild the site for supreme functionality. Jim and I said, "Okay, you're our man."

His first excuse for why the initial phase of the work was not completed on time seemed legitimate, spinning around in your car on wet pavement at fifty-five miles an hour is traumatic. Thankfully, he was not hurt. But the excuses continued. Without a knowledge of website coding, we were at his mercy. Four months into the rebuild, we were shocked at how little had actually been accomplished. Failing time and time again to meet deadlines and keep his word, Jim and I realized we couldn't afford to have him be a part of our team because we couldn't trust him to do what he said he would do.

We wished him all the best and went our separate ways.

THE CHANNEL OF TRUST

If we all just did what we said, would I even need to be writing about trust? When we say I trust someone aren't we really just saying I trust them to do what they say? The answer is yes, but it involves much more than that. It involves whatever has been entrusted to the other person in the relationship and the expectation that it will be delivered, honored, and protected. When I am hired to give a keynote, event planners are entrusting me with the success and reputation of their event. They are trusting that I will deliver a message that will be a benefit to their audience. Between two people in any given relationship there exists what I call the *channel of trust* wherein flow all the expectations and promises for the relationship. Likewise, in every organization this same *channel of trust* exists between the leaders and those who perform the work assigned to them. The employees are entrusted by the supervisors with specific job descriptions and duties; the supervisors are entrusted to provide everything the employees need to do the work, and both the supervisor and the employee are trusted to be everything they said they would be in the interview.

When all these expectations and promises have been clearly stated there is less chance of a dispute when they are violated. I once accepted a job offer solely because I was promised by the manager that I would be groomed to take their place when they retire in one year. When one year came and went, it became clear the she had no intention of leaving which was a violation of what I considered to be a promise. She did not deny the promise was made but she wasn't able to say when she would fulfill it. So I had a decision to make, and I ultimately chose to go work for another company. Incidentally, at the writing of this book the manager is still there.

AREA OF UNSPOKEN EXPECTATIONS

But some expectations and promises live outside the boundaries of what has been clearly stated, and this is where trust is often broken. Everything that people expect or want out of the relationship cannot be spoken or put in a job description or written in an employee manual. In this gray area differences in age and experience, in personality, in upbringing, in expectations, in opinions of what is right and fair, and more can come into play. I call this the *area of unspoken expectations*. For example, an employee might expect their supervisor to take good care to guide them to a better future, but the expectation is never stated, it is just assumed the supervisor thinks the same. So it is not always the case that trust is broken because someone had a malicious or selfish intent. It is often the result of different expectations that were never clearly communicated or because there were different interpretations of events.

THE COST OF BROKEN TRUST

We often think about trust as being destroyed by one fatal blow; it is definitely very dramatic and translates well on the big screen that way. In the movie *Braveheart*, Mel Gibson plays William Wallace, a Scotsman who leads his fellow countrymen into war against England. There is a battle scene where Wallace's forces are greatly outnumbered by the English, and they are beaten badly. With the battle already won by the English, Wallace chases down an opposing soldier. In their duel both get knocked off their horses. Wallace gains the advantage and pulls off his opponent's steel mask and discovers it is Robert the Bruce, a Scottish Baron who had pledged his support to fight with the Scots in the battle but actually betrayed Wallace and fought for the English. Gibson's acting is brilliant, as the discovery that Bruce is his enemy literally knocks him on his backside, as the sword of betrayal pierces his heart.

In reality, the death of trust comes not by one fatal blow, nor is it a death by a thousand cuts, but somewhere in between. Each missed deadline by my web designer to deliver work was a blow to the trust between us, and eventually the fatal blow was delivered. There were a lot of unspoken expectations which, in hindsight, I would have done a better job of uncovering and getting out into the open. It is wise to voice all your expectations and ask for the other person to share their expectations as well before every endeavor.

But all is not necessarily lost when trust first starts to come off the rails. Conversations can and should be had to find out why things are going the way they are, to communicate unspoken expectations, and make adjustments if needed. I find most people are very understanding and want the relationship to work. As it relates to companies and employees, I've already written about all that goes into hiring an employee and the high cost to find a replacement if they leave. No company wants to go through that process more than we have to and incur those costs. This provides motivation to do all in our power to restore trust.

We want to do everything we can to maintain trust because once the trust that was originally established is destroyed, it is gone forever. When the North and

South towers of the World Trade Center collapsed on September 11, 2001, they came down in an avalanche of dust and debris. Those towers could never be rebuilt with the same material that now lay in a twisted pile. All new construction material had to be used to build the one Freedom Tower that now stands in their place. In addition, it was a long and difficult process as people struggled to agree on what the finished product should look like. If trust is destroyed, a new trust can be built in its place, but it will never be what it was before.

The death of trust usually means the death of the relationship. Some relationships, like basic friendships, allow for people to simply part ways because there is nothing that binds them together other than their choice to be friends. Companies and employees can choose to part ways, but again, that comes with a very high price that we would like to avoid if at all possible.

But what do you do when trust is broken and you can't just choose to never see each other again? What happens when trust is broken and you still have to work together? This is the case when a husband and wife divorce and still share custody of their children, or when two people work for the same company, and they have to work together. Working without trust is unworkable. It is certain to produce an inferior product or result and innocent bystanders can get caught in the crossfire.

WHEN A LEADER FAILS TO PROTECT HIS TEAM, IT IS A VIOLATION OF TRUST.

A friend of mine is a salesperson in a retail store. A new employee was hired to process orders, arrange customer deliveries, and other general duties at the store. But there is a problem, the new employee is toxic! She is the athlete in the locker room who causes strife and dissension, and it is clear that is all she will ever be. She is affecting the ability of the sales staff to do their job, and because they are paid on a commission basis, this is not a personal issue but a livelihood issue. The girl has got to go!

But there is another problem: the supervisor is not addressing the situation. He himself has witnessed her behavior along with hearing how bad it is from his employees, but...nothing. Her behavior continues unchecked, and until she hears from the person who had the power to hire her, and therefore, has the power to fire her, she will continue in her ways. Every day the supervisor fails to act, the more his employees feel betrayed. When the leader does not protect his team, it becomes a violation of trust.

MY WORK WITH LEADERS IS TO INCREASE THEIR TRUST FACTOR.

Employee surveys reveal that the three things employees want most from an employer is a relationship with their supervisor, development, and open and honest communication. Necessary to all three of these is a trusted supervisor. That is why the essence of my work with leaders is to help them develop the traits and actions that build trust between them and their employees. I call it the supervisor's *trust factor*. I am not saying they are untrustworthy leaders that need to be made trustworthy. Rather, what can happen is the leader's trustworthiness remains hidden behind a lack of communication, or it sits buried beneath tasks where there is no time to develop meaningful relationships with their employees.

Let me say that the *channel of trust* flows both ways between the supervisor and the employee. All the responsibility does not rest on the supervisor to make the relationship work. The purpose of this book is to help companies retain their most valuable asset, their employees, but that doesn't mean you want to retain all of them. When an employee proves to be untrustworthy it is good business to terminate their employment. But for those we want to keep, it is the leaders that establish and maintain the level of trust in an organization. An *Employee Engagement Environment* that is characterized by trust will have the following elements:

- Employees who trust the leaders of the company to create a dynamic working environment that looks out for them.
- Co-workers who trust each other and have each other's backs.
- Leaders who trust their employees to make decisions and take actions that benefit the company and their customers.

CHARACTER IS THE SEED OF TRUST.

No discussion of trust is complete without talking about character. If trust is the tree, character is the seed. You can't have one without the other. Character is the condition that makes trust possible. A person can fake it for a while, but eventually their character will be revealed. I said something earlier in this book that bears repeating, for *Retention Architecture* to work, it requires heart, a genuine care and concern for your fellow man! Only a leader with character can be trusted to:

- be just and fair
- look out for the interest of others
- put others before themselves
- act with integrity
- be honest even when it costs him something
- give credit where credit is due
- admit he doesn't have the answer

OUTSTANDING CHARACTER IS AVAILABLE TO ALL.

Character informs every other thing. Character influences everything it touches. It guides what it is holding. Outstanding character uses a thing for the purpose for which it was made, a gun, a knife, a car, a computer, even the human body. What is the proper use of the human body? Outstanding character will find it. The positive or negative use of a thing is in the hands of the one who possesses it. The mind of a genius, possessed by a man of outstanding character, is a force for good.

Unlike other desirable attributes, outstanding character is available to all. It does not discriminate like other attributes do. If a man's arm strength is such that he cannot throw a baseball faster than seventy miles an hour, he will never have outstanding pitching abilities, and a pitching career in the major leagues is out of the question. But an outstanding character is available to all who want it, who desire it, the weak and the strong, the short and the tall, the young and the old. You will have to tame the passions, develop self-control, learn to deny the good for the best. It will come with a price, but it will be worth it!

What has more value, a rose or a clump of crabgrass?

A diamond or a rock from the driveway? Beethoven's *Moonlight Sonata* or the sound of my cat walking over the piano keys? These questions don't require a response. The answers are self-evident. What has more value, a man of outstanding character or a man without?

BEN FRANKLIN'S PURSUIT OF MORAL PERFECTION

I first became aware of Ben Franklin's pursuit of moral perfection when Jim, listening to the audio version of the *Autobiography of Benjamin Franklin*, shared it with me. Throughout his life, Franklin was always working to improve himself. His efforts were obviously rewarded when you look at his achievements, becoming a successful printer, scientist, musician, author, and diplomat.

In his autobiography, Franklin writes of one of his most ambitious attempts at self-improvement.

"I conceiv'd the bold and arduous project of arriving at moral perfection. I wish'd to live without committing any fault at any time; I would conquer all that either natural inclination, custom, or company might lead me into."

Franklin committed to living true to these thirteen virtues as they were written in his book:

- **Temperance**: Eat not to dullness; drink not to elevation.
- **Silence**: Speak not but what may benefit others or yourself; avoid trifling conversation.
- **Order**: Let all your things have their places; let each part of your business have its time.
- **Resolution**: Resolve to perform what you ought; perform without fail what you resolve.

- **Frugality**: Make no expense but to do good to others or yourself; i.e., waste nothing.
- **Industry**: Lose no time; be always employed in something useful; cut off all unnecessary actions.
- **Sincerity**: Use no hurtful deceit; think innocently and justly, and, if you speak, speak accordingly.
- **Justice**: Wrong none by doing injuries, or omitting the benefits that are your duty.
- **Moderation**: Avoid extremes; forbear resenting injuries so much as you think they deserve.
- **Cleanliness**: Tolerate no uncleanliness in body, clothes, or habitation.
- **Tranquility**: Be not disturbed at trifles, or at accidents common or unavoidable.
- **Chastity**: Rarely use venery but for health or offspring, never to dullness, weakness, or the injury of your own or another's peace or reputation.
- **Humility**: Imitate Jesus and Socrates.

Franklin carried a chart and he would score himself at the end of each day, placing a dot next to those virtues he violated. How long he continued this practice I do not know, but over time he saw that the number of dots did decrease. Obviously, Franklin was unable to do the impossible and achieve his goal of moral perfection, but he did say he was a better man for it.

When reading through the thirteen virtues Franklin listed along with their descriptions, I experience a calibration of sorts. I sense myself wanting to move toward the standard being set and to live up to it. When I hear "speak not but what may benefit others or yourself; avoid trifling conversation," the words seem so self-evidently true and right that I experience an adjustment, an alignment, like when I go to the chiropractor and he gives my back a good cracking.

Finding out that Franklin even thought he could live the perfect moral life, I had to chuckle and chalk it up to the idealism of youth, seeing that he began his attempt at the age of twenty. But by making perfection his goal, he was certain to make progress. In golf, there is an approach to the game called "aim small, miss small." It is the approach that pro golfer Jordan Spieth used to win The Masters, the British Open, and the US Open. The idea is simple, the smaller target you pick out, the smaller your miss is going to be. For instance, rather than aim at one side of the fairway, you aim at a very specific part of the fairway. Applied to our discussion of character, there is no smaller target you can aim at than perfection.

When I got up to write this morning, I was first getting organized and I found another Donald Miller video in my email inbox. Donald Miller is the author of *Building a Storybrand*, a book I highly recommend for helping you to clarify your marketing message. His video message this morning was about being a good person. Donald recently heard JoAnne Rogers talking about her late husband, Fred Rogers, who is in the news because of the new movie, *It's a Beautiful Day in the Neighborhood*. Among other things, she said Fred had to work at being a nice person. Intrigued, I went online and read where Tom Hanks, who plays Fred in the movie, said something similar. Hanks said that he grew up understanding kindness was a choice. When we meet people of outstanding character, we might be tempted to think that they came to it naturally, that they are just nice people by nature. But the truth is they made a conscious decision to work on it.

I have a few final thoughts about character. George Bailey, the fictional character in the movie *It's a Wonderful Life*, made several decisions in the crucible of his life that determined, not only his character, but the character of the whole town he lived in. George ends up facing bankruptcy, scandal, and jail time, all because his Uncle Billy loses a large deposit of money that will put the Bailey Building and Loan out of business. As his life comes crashing down around him, George says to Clarence, the guardian angel sent to save him, that he wishes he'd never been born. This gives Clarence an idea...he will show George what life would have been like for Bedford Falls and the people there if he hadn't been born. What George discovers is that the character of the town and his friends and family were completely different. Everyone's character changed for the worse because George wasn't there to positively influence the world around him.

A person is their character. Each person's character touches the lives of so many others. But an organization has a character also; it is a collective character where each individual's character is plugged into an equation that no one has figured out yet, that then equals the organization's collective character. A good character is available to any organization, but it will need to decide to have it, and then work as a team to achieve it. When one person's character in the organization improves, the whole organization improves. It will come with a price, but it will be worth it!

FOR FURTHER REFLECTION

Most likely, everyone has had trust broken in a relationship at one time or another, so the discussion points in this chapter are likely familiar, but reflecting on trust and character from an organizational position is valuable. Take time to reflect on the trust level in your organization, within the relationships between employees themselves, and employees and their supervisors or managers. Consider what improvements might help shift the dominant mindset forward.

1. Describe what you believe the promises and expectations are that flow in the *channel of trust* between you and your team members. Between you and the company…

2. Should more grace and understanding be practiced when there are violations of unspoken expectations, and if so, why?

3. Describe a situation where you were able to restore trust before it was completely destroyed. What did you do to turn things around?

4. What are your impressions of Benjamin Franklin's list of 13 virtues? Would you consider them to be timeless?

5. Describe the collective character of your organization.

Chapter 8

Empathy and Recognition

We don't come to the world as unbiased reporters; we see it through a lens of our own making. Sometimes I see the world through a filter of frustrations, of successes, through failures, through dreams. The amount of light entering my lens can be dependent on what is happening in my life at that moment. If I'm experiencing success, I see the world as a fertile field that rewards hard work, if there are only obstacles, I see dry rocky dirt. My desire is to always see a fertile field, even when I'm facing obstacles. I'm working on that.

Ken Keyes Jr. took it to another level when he said, "A loving person lives in a loving world. A hostile person lives in a hostile world. Everyone you meet is your mirror." Who we are determines how we see others. If you value love, you will love others. If you value good, you will see the good in others.

This presents a kind of chicken and egg situation. Does a person love because they were first loved by another? Are they unfriendly because the world was first unfriendly to them? The question is not a useless one. People often experience a true transformation of mindset only after they have identified the events that caused their thinking in the first place and the subsequent decision they made to deal with it. This allows them to come to it more truthfully and make a different choice.

We each have a lifetime of experiences, decisions, and habits that have shaped who we are, and these determine how we see others. Our challenge is and has always been to see ourselves honestly. We are notorious for spotting the faults of others while ignoring our own. We have a mirror to fix our hair in but no mirror for the heart. Unless you ask Keyes who says "everyone we meet is our mirror." When I come to the bathroom mirror in the morning I see a face not ready for prime time. But after some care and attention I'm ready to face the world. Much of this book is about what a leader wants to see when they look in the mirrors of others, and what care and attention they can apply so they are ready to lead in their world.

When I consider the pool of people who remain after the hopelessly and helplessly bad have been removed, I believe people express enough goodness that if we want to see the good we will, and they express enough bad that if we want to see the bad we will. The question before each one of us is do you want to live in a hostile world or a loving world?

EMPLOYEES ARE YOUR FIRST CUSTOMERS.

Your business is providing either a product or service to your customers. Without customers you don't have a business. Without employees you can't provide your product or service to your customers. Customers and employees are equally important, so it makes good business sense to treat them that way.

In the cases where they aren't treated equally, it is usually the customer who gets more love than the employee. The reason for this has to do with the flow of money. We tend to value the hand that gives us money more than we value the hand we give money to.

When you pay your employees, is your thinking: *I pay you, so you have work to do,"* or is it *"You've done work for me, so I'm paying you"*? This is not just semantics; it reflects two different relationships you might have with your employees. I would argue that the second mindset will help you value your employees as much as you value your customers.

So how do you keep your employees on an equal footing with your customers? Give them what they want! That's what you do for your customers, so do the same for your employees. And it isn't any secret what they want. They have been surveyed so many times that it is no mystery.

Here is a list of seven wants that consistently show up on employee surveys:

- Competitive pay and benefits
- A clear understanding of their role and what is expected of them
- Upward mobility and development opportunities
- Recognition
- Trusted and approachable leadership
- Flexibility in work schedule
- Open and honest communication

I FEEL YOUR PAIN

In 1992, George H.W. Bush, the father of George W. Bush, was finishing up his first term as President of the United States. In his re-election bid he was being challenged by Bill Clinton, the candidate for the Democrat party, and Ross Perot who ran as a third-party candidate.

In the second debate, a young woman stood up and asked the following question, "How has the national debt affected each of your lives, and if it hasn't, how can you honestly find a cure for the economic problems of the common people if you have no experience in what's ailing them?" The question was somewhat adjusted a few moments later by the debate moderator to include the personal effects of the recession on each of the candidates.

After Perot had answered, Bush stood up and said "I think the national debt affects everybody." He was quickly interrupted by the questioner "You, on a personal basis?" It only went downhill from there. Bush even asked for clarification, almost challenging the questioner by asking whether she was saying that rich people aren't affected by the debt and the recession. The woman explained that she had friends who had trouble paying their mortgages or car payments. "How can you help us if you don't know what we're feeling." By the end of his answer Bush voters were a bit deflated and concerned, recognizing how that wasn't one of the president's best moments.

That concern would only increase as Bill Clinton stepped toward the questioner and asked her, "How has it affected you again? And then he answered his own question restating what she had previously said. Then he answered, "I've been governor of a small state for twelve years. I'll tell you how it's affected me. Every year, Congress and the president sign laws that make us do more things and give us less money to do it. I see middle-class people whose services have gone down while the wealthy have gotten tax cuts. When people lose their jobs, there is a good chance I know them by their name. If the factory closes, I know the people who ran it."

Regardless of which candidate you supported or which candidate's economic policies would actually be better for the woman who asked the question, there was no doubting that Clinton had won the exchange. Rightly or wrongly, Bush came off as detached, unable to relate. For Clinton, this has been referred to as his "I feel your pain" moment. He demonstrated empathy which is just what the questioner was looking for.

EMPATHY

Politics can be an ungenuine business, and with this last story, I risk rousing the reader's partisanship which could distract from seeing that empathy has just been introduced to the stage. When I did an online search for the most important traits for good leadership, several lists came up, and empathy never topped a single one. In fact, empathy only made an appearance on a little over half of all the lists I viewed. But I have to tell you, sometimes I think I could make empathy the star of the show. Theodore Roosevelt is quoted as saying "Nobody cares how much you know until they know how much you care." Many of the things employees want happen within the context of a relationship with a supervisor who genuinely cares for them. Caring for another person is not possible without empathy. When I work with leaders one-on-one or in groups the predominant challenges and issues center around relationships. You will recall that within the *Employee Engagement Environment*, employees are evaluating everything and asking themselves *Do I still want to work here?* If the company's leaders are not empathizing with their employees, those employees are far more likely to answer, *No, I don't want to work here anymore.*

WHAT IS EMPATHY?

Empathy is the ability to understand the needs of others and to be mindful of their feelings and thoughts concerning their day-to-day challenges. You don't have to agree with how they are thinking or feeling; it just means you are willing and able to appreciate and understand their experience.

I was on a coaching call with a sales manager when he started to express frustrations he was having with his supervisor who was making decisions that were negatively affecting the performance of his team. With each question I asked and with each answer he gave we peeled back the onion until he eventually identified a significant misunderstanding they had that resulted in a loss of trust. His supervisor had incorrectly thought he was responsible for a mishap, and when he was able to show the situation wasn't his doing, they still weren't able to return to the great relationship they once had. All he could see was someone who was still holding him responsible for something he hadn't done. I told him, for the sake of the company and the relationship, to get outside of his own interpretation of events and try to understand what his supervisor might be thinking and feeling. Everything his supervisor did that was supposedly to get back at him had another explanation, if he was willing to consider it.

Some of the benefits of empathy in your organization that ultimately lead to a better relationship between the supervisor and employee:

- At the end of the day, supervisors are expected to get results, and the pressure to produce in a highly competitive marketplace can create a very results driven culture. Empathy allows supervisors to not lose sight of employee needs and the quality of their work experience as they push for results.
- When leaders practice empathy with their team members they can expect empathy in return. Reasonable people are usually ready to reciprocate with an expression of generosity when it has first been expressed to them.
- Empathetic leaders are better listeners, which allows them to discover issues that otherwise might have gone undetected.
- Empathetic leaders are able to put the thoughts and feelings of their employees on an equal footing with their own. The result is that employees feel more valued and appreciated.
- Empathy equips the supervisor with more patience to deal with the struggles certain employees might experience. This increases the overall performance of their team as no one gets left behind.
- Empathy builds trust between the supervisor and the employee when the employee realizes they have a supervisor who is able to understand and appreciate all they go through to perform their job.

One final thought before empathy exits the stage. To understand how others might be feeling we can often just turn to ourselves. We are all made from the same stuff. We might be shaped and seasoned and put together a little differently, but our essential ingredients are the same. Therefore, many of our experiences and deepest longings we have in common. Look to your wants and needs to better understand others. And then treat them the way you would want to be treated.

RECOGNITION AND APPRECIATION: THE HUMAN NEED TO BELONG

It is through the power of story that we often learn the virtues of life and are moved to practice them. I first became aware of Sister Helen P. Mrosla's true story through one of John Maxwell's books. It so moved me that I figured, if it inspires me, it will inspire others. I have told this story a number of times from the speaker's platform, and I have yet to meet a room that wasn't moved by its message. Sister Helen was a teacher at Saint Mary's school in Morris, Minnesota. I pick up her story at its midpoint.

> *One Friday, things just didn't feel right.*
> *We had worked hard on a new concept all*
> *week, and I sensed that the students were*
> *frowning, frustrated with themselves—*
> *and edgy with one another. I had to stop*
> *this crankiness before it got out of hand.*
> *So I asked them to list the names of the*
> *other students in the room on two sheets*
> *of paper, leaving a space between each*
> *name. Then I told them to think of the*

nicest thing they could say about each of their classmates and write it down. It took the remainder of the class period to finish the assignment, and as the students left the room, each one handed me the papers. Charlie smiled. Mark said, "Thank you for teaching me, Sister. Have a good weekend."

That Saturday, I wrote down the name of each student on a separate sheet of paper, and I listed what everyone else had said about that individual. On Monday I gave each student his or her list. Before long, the entire class was smiling. "Really?" I heard whispered. "I never knew that meant anything to anyone!" "I didn't know others liked me so much!" No one ever mentioned those papers in class again. I never knew if they discussed them after class or with their parents, but it didn't matter. The exercise had accomplished its purpose. The students were happy with themselves and one another again.

That group of students moved on. Several years later, after I returned from vacation, my parents met me at the airport. As we were driving home, Mother asked me the usual questions about the trip—the weather, my experiences in general. There was a light lull in the conversation.

*Mother gave Dad a sideways glance
and simply said, "Dad?" My father
cleared his throat as he usually did before
something important. "The Eklunds
called last night," he began. "Really?" I
said. "I haven't heard from them in years.
I wonder how Mark is. "Dad responded
quietly. "Mark was killed in Vietnam," he
said. "The funeral is tomorrow, and his
parents would like it if you could attend."
To this day I can still point to the exact
spot on I-494 where Dad told me about
Mark.*

*I had never seen a serviceman in a
military coffin before. Mark looked so
handsome, so mature. The church was
packed with Mark's friends. Chuck's sister
sang "The Battle Hymn of the Republic."
Why did it have to rain on the day of
the funeral? It was difficult enough at
the graveside. The pastor said the usual
prayers, and the bugler played taps. One
by one those who loved Mark took a last
walk by the coffin and sprinkled it with
holy water.*

*I was the last one to bless the coffin. As
I stood there, one of the soldiers who
had acted as pallbearer came up to me.
"Were you Mark's math teacher?" he
asked. I nodded as I continued to stare
at the coffin. "Mark talked about you a*

lot," he said.

After the funeral, most of Mark's former classmates headed to Chuck's farmhouse for lunch. Mark's mother and father were there, obviously waiting for me. "We want to show you something," his father said, taking a wallet out of his pocket. "They found this on Mark when he was killed. We thought you might recognize it." Opening the billfold, he carefully removed two worn pieces of notebook paper that had obviously been taped, folded and refolded many times. I knew without looking that the papers were the ones on which I had listed all the good things each of Mark's classmates had said about him.

"Thank you so much for doing that," Mark's mother said. "As you can see, Mark treasured it." Mark's classmates started to gather around us. Charlie smiled rather sheepishly and said, "I still have my list. It's in the top drawer of my desk at home." Chuck's wife said, "Chuck asked me to put this in our wedding album." "I have mine too," Marilyn said. "It's in my diary." Then Vicki, another classmate, reached into her pocketbook, took out her wallet and showed her worn and frazzled list to the group. "I carry this with me at all times," Vicki said, without batting an eyelash. "I think we all saved

*our lists." That's when I finally sat down
and cried. I cried for Mark and for all his
friends who would never see him again.*

Sister Helen's story took place fifty years ago, but it is still relevant today. What would make so many adults hold on to pieces of paper they had received years before as kids, some of them carrying those pages with them everywhere they went, even to battle in a foreign land halfway around the world? The top layer of the answer is that everyone is hungry for appreciation and recognition. But underneath is the human need to belong, to be a part of something. When we are recognized we feel accepted, believing that our existence has meaning and purpose.

THE LEADERSHIP GAME

I have facilitated numerous team-building sessions within companies using a John Maxwell created tool called the Leadership Game. This is a fun and interactive game that inspires dialogue which, among other things, identifies what the organization is doing well and what could be done better. The game also brings about a time for edifying one another. Through a series of directives and questions, employees take the opportunity to thank and acknowledge each other. One such exercise is where each player writes the name of every other player on a separate Post-it® Note along with a leadership characteristic they admire about them. They are then directed to deliver each Post-it® Note to the place where each person is sitting. Once they have all read their individual notes, I ask them each to share the one that meant the most to them. During this game, previously unexpressed thoughts and feelings are shared that are often way overdue. I've seen tears. I've seen walls of anger and competitiveness fall down to be replaced by understanding and forgiveness.

IF YOU'VE GOT SOMETHING GOOD TO SAY, SAY IT

My dad never meets a stranger. Do you remember the character Tim Conway created for the Carol Burnett Show in the 1970s? The shaggy white-haired old man who moved with short slow steps? When you walk like that, which my dad does, you have time to make friends.

My dad always has a compliment, and he is not stingy with them. He lets people know. I love my dad, and I love that about him! So I try to be like him in this way. One day I had a nice thought about a person who was before me, and I started to walk away without sharing it. But I caught myself, and the spirit of my dad rose up in me and I told them. They smiled and seemed to appreciate what I said.

You've heard the saying, if you've got nothing good to say then don't say it. True. And if you've got something good to say, then say it. Our good thoughts do far more good when the world gets to hear them! Likewise, if you have something worth recognizing and appreciating about an employee or supervisor, by all means say it.

LEADERS FACILITATE RECOGNITION

I am a facilitator. I create the conditions so connections can be made and communication can occur. One of my favorite things to do, because it is so meaningful, is to gather a roomful of people together in a circle and facilitate a time of recognition. I always did this when I was the drama director at my church. After a big production, where so many volunteers had contributed their time to create something amazing for our audience, I would pull everyone together and, one by one, go around the circle and acknowledge and thank each person for their unique contribution. I never struggled to find something specific to say about each person because I had been observing and appreciating their work from the very start. It meant so much to them that I was able to share in detail the work they had done!

I recently facilitated a similar time of recognition for a company where I trained thirty of their leaders. When the six-month training was completed, the owners hosted a dinner party for the leaders and their family members to congratulate and recognize them for a job well done! I was asked to give a certificate to each person who completed the training, and I suggested we say something about each one of them. (I never let a good opportunity to recognize slip away.)

During our six months together, I had taken notes on each leader's involvement and progress in the training and these notes proved useful when preparing my remarks, allowing me to be specific in what I recognized. Without much planning as to exactly how this would be done, I stood at the front of the room and said the first person's name. Unprompted, that person came and stood by my side. This was even better because now I was able to interact with them, which gave them the opportunity to speak and to recognize what the company and the owners meant to them; and also gave their fellow leaders in the audience the opportunity to acknowledge them. This set the pattern and the remaining twenty-nine leaders did just the same! Some very meaningful and heartfelt thoughts were expressed that night!

THINGS TO KEEP IN MIND WHEN GIVING RECOGNITION:

• Employees want to be recognized for what is truly deserving of recognition, otherwise it comes off as insincere and self-serving.
• Employees want to be recognized for a specific action. Continually hearing general statements of recognition like "you did a nice job today" can even work against you.
• Encourage peer-to-peer recognition. This will pick up some of the things you miss.
• Recognition is best when it is done immediately, when it is fresh.

THE BENEFITS OF RECOGNITION:

• Employees get something they want. This helps retain them.
• Employees feel like they belong and are making a contribution.
• When leaders publicly recognize employees, all the employees' level of trust increases for the leader because they see that they can trust him to share the credit.
• When leaders adopt a lifestyle of spontaneous recognition, the engagement level of the employees increases along with the job satisfaction.
• Recognition creates a more supportive and enjoyable place to work.

FOR FURTHER REFLECTION

Every employee wants to be valued for their contributions. Consider the following questions as you reflect on your focus on being empathetic to your employees and recognizing them for their authentic contributions.

1. Describe your impressions of Key Keyes Jr.'s quote, "A loving person lives in a loving world. A hostile person lives in a hostile world. Everyone you meet is your mirror."

2. How important is it for organizations to treat their employees with the same importance as they treat their customers?

3. Think of a time when you had empathy for a person's circumstances. How did that change your relationship with them and the way you viewed their situation?

4. Describe a time when you recognized a person for something good they did or said where you could see it meant a lot to them. What do you think they were feeling?

Chapter 9

Develop Your
Employees

If the majority of the people who work for your company consider you to be an *Insignificant* or *Temporary* employer, you are hemorrhaging employees. This makes it very difficult to keep and deliver on the customer and client promises you are making through your marketing statements. You will recall that your marketing statements are born out of your *Business Image Ideal*. This ideal represents the very best you have to offer the people who do business with you. If you are trapped in the cycle of losing employees and replacing them, then many of your staff are new and not up to speed. When the number of new hires, defined as employees who have been with your company for less than one year, reaches a critical mass, there will be a drop-off in company performance, and you will experience a *Business Image Shortfall*.

That's what happened at ABC, the company for which I was hired to complete an internal investigation, which I mentioned in the introduction. Through their commitment to service, dependability, and safety, they had established themselves as an industry leader. This was accomplished in large part by their ability to retain experienced and knowledgeable staff. But they had lost that edge by the time I came on the scene, evidenced by the fact that twenty-two of the forty-three people I interviewed for the investigation had been with the company for less than one year. With that many new employees, ABCs hard-earned reputation for dependability and quality was slowly eroding.

EMPLOYEES WANT TRAINING AND DEVELOPMENT

In the talent acquisition chapter of this book, we looked at how you could attract and hire employees who have the personality traits that will help you live up to your *Business Image Ideal*. In this chapter we are looking at what you do with employees after you have hired them so you can live up to your ideal. For that I take you back to the *Employee Engagement Environment*.

You will recall that in the *Integration* stage within the *Employee Engagement Environment*, your employees are evaluating everything about your organization. And many of them are asking, where can I go with this company? Where is the opportunity for upward mobility and advancement? What new skills will I develop, and what new training will I receive that will make me a more valuable employee and help me achieve more in my career? Once I'm fully integrated, what is my true earnings potential with this company? This is all very important to them. Top performers will not be content to enter into your organization and have nowhere else to go. When upward mobility and development is limited then you can be certain that they will have a *Temporary* mindset about your organization, and you will only serve as a steppingstone to a better opportunity, assuming you are able to hire them at all.

But development and upward mobility is not just the desire of high achievers, most all employees want it. It consistently ranks in the top ten things that employees look for in an employer. This is a good thing! You want employees who have an upward mindset. It is the very thing that keeps them engaged and productive and appreciating in value. As long as you keep developing them, giving them more responsibility, giving them opportunities to lead and have greater influence and impact, they are more likely to stay with your organization. Zig Ziglar has a well-known quote that I have repeated from the speaker's platform more times than I can count. "You can have everything in life you want, if you will just help enough other people get what they want." Therein lies the key. By giving your employees the development and training they want, in return you get an experienced and knowledgeable workforce that is able to keep the promises you make to your customers in your marketing statements. `

As an employee I always wanted to know where I could go within an organization and what new tasks they could give me. That was the case when I worked at a quasi-state agency. I had been with the organization for one year, acting as a recruiter in the HR department, when the agency decided to create a new HR director position; this person's responsibility would be overseeing the HR department. Before the director came on board, that responsibility was carried out by the HR manager. When the new director arrived he sent out an email request to every member of the department, wanting to know what duties in our job descriptions we actually performed, what duties we were performing that weren't in our job descriptions, and what would each of us like to do that we weren't currently doing.

Over the next couple weeks, he and I met in person more than once. During these meetings he asked what my strengths were, what I liked and did not like about working at the agency, what would I change, and what additional training would I like to receive. I explained to him that the organization had no onboarding program to speak of, and without it, we were failing to meet the needs of our new hires at a very critical time in our relationship with them. Not long after that he asked me to head a small team of three other people to create an onboarding program for the organization. Within two months my team and I were able to create that program. Now, we had a process that would make new hires feel more welcomed and valued.

Our new director was smart. He asked me what I thought the organization needed and then gave me the autonomy to make it happen. I was engaged in my work and glad for the opportunity to use my leadership skills. Creating this program equipped me with knowledge I didn't have before that increased my value to this organization and any other I might work for in the future. In fact, I implemented this very same program for my next employer.

A PARENT'S INTEREST IN YOUR EMPLOYEES?

I have two sons who are eighteen months apart in age. As their mother, I want to see them realize their full potential and live productive and accomplished lives. Therefore, I have always made it my purpose to speak possibility into their lives. So when they were freshmen and sophomores in high school, I planted the seed in their minds that they could graduate at the top of their class. I wasn't being pie in the sky. Having homeschooled them for many years, I recognized they had the intelligence. And it was a smaller school, so they didn't have as many kids to beat out. If they made it a goal and applied themselves accordingly, I believed they had a legitimate chance.

The first time I mentioned it they didn't give me any reason to think they agreed or disagreed with my assessment. I think they were just processing what I was saying. As the semesters passed and the school assembled for Awards Day each year, they kept showing up near the top. That's when I would remind them that with more intention and hard work they could take over the top spot.

As it turned out, my oldest son graduated as the valedictorian of his class, and two years later, his younger brother was the salutatorian of his class. When I first planted the seed in their minds, they probably had no idea what it would mean to them. It was too far away. But when it happened, I know it meant a lot to them. It is an accomplishment they will always have that they can pull out to remind themselves that they have what it takes.

Is it possible for you to have the same level of desire to see your employees succeed that a parent has for their children? Probably not. But we can still do many of the same things. I didn't leave it up my sons to see the opportunity that was before them. I made sure to identify what was possible. You can do the same with your employees. Make clear what is available and show them the path to get there. If you see potential in some specific area, encourage and develop that area. They don't always see it in themselves. Many are trying to find their way in life, and they can benefit from your insight and experience.

When you take a sincere interest in developing your employees to be the best they can be, you can expect their loyalty in return. Yes, you could develop them to the point that they become attractive to other companies and you lose them. But that is a risk worth taking. Keep finding new ways to develop them and give them reasons to stay. Every year that you hold on to a valuable employee adds up to a greater return on your investment in them.

There is a quote by Robert Baden-Powell, the founder of the worldwide Boy Scout movement, "Try and leave this world a little better than you found it, and when your turn comes to die, you can die happy in feeling that at any rate, you have not wasted your time but have done your best." For the sake of our discussion, I have modified the quote to address the employers and supervisors of the world. "Try and leave your employees better off than when you found them and when, if ever, they decide to leave, you can wish them well, happy you have not wasted the opportunity to help them be their best."

THE CONFIDENCE OF COMPETENCE

Recently, Jim and I were out to dinner with some old friends. It was with Dan Holland and his wife Beth. You might remember Dan was the pastor of Metro Church who hired me to be the director of the church drama ministry. Dan retired from the ministry and is now North America Director of Operations at a wonderful company called Softwash Systems founded by Dan's and my good friend, AC Lockyer.

We had all spent the day at Softwashapolooza, the Softwash annual conference where they appreciate and develop the many people who work internationally under the Softwash banner. Dan hired me to give my keynote based on the material in this book, to facilitate a conflict resolution workshop and to sit on the "Ask the HR Expert" panel.

It had been a number of years since we had seen Dan and Beth, and Beth was asking me questions about my business. She then asked Jim if he still enjoyed teaching guitar after all these years. He answered yes, saying he enjoys it more now than at any other time before. He explained that after so many years dedicated to playing and teaching, he has developed many insights and methods to approaching the guitar that he loves passing on to his students. He is able to do his job very well, which is a source of confidence and joy. Jim was describing what we all experience when we do something very well. I call it the *Confidence of Competence*. Our competence gives birth to confidence.

The *Confidence of Competence* is one of the best things you can give your employees. It will be a source of deep satisfaction for them. When you have a well-trained and competent employee, this is just some of what you will see:

- They possess thorough product and service knowledge.
- They are familiar and proficient with all equipment, software, and tools needed to perform their job.
- They can troubleshoot a problem and fix it.

- They can adapt and perform their job in changing environments.
- Guided by knowledge, they perform faster and more efficiently.
- They know what questions to ask.
- They have the answers to their customers' questions.

As their competence increases, their confidence grows. When their confidence is in full bloom this is just some of what you will see:

- They are the best version of themselves.
- They have more energy that wasn't wasted on self-doubt.
- They remain calm and in control when events don't go as planned.
- They are a source of contagious confidence for their fellow team members.
- They move with purpose, undistracted by uncertainty.
- Customers sense their confidence which creates trust.
- They remain determined in the face of adversity.
- Their self-belief allows them to lead and take initiative.

GIVE YOUR TASKS AWAY FOR GREATER RETURNS

When I go into companies and work with their supervisors, it's not uncommon to hear that supervisors are working sixty-hour weeks and are on the edge of burnout. And I tell them this, if you'll do this one thing, you'll get three things in return. What is it? Give your tasks away. I ask supervisors to list all the tasks they do, identify the three tasks only they can do, and start giving the rest away to their employees. And what do they get in return?

- Engaged and satisfied employees.
- Time to develop relationships with their employees.
- They get their life back.

CROSS TRAINING

We counted twenty-six pine trees in our yard before we recently had five removed. Three different reputable tree removal companies bid on the job, and we went with the lowest bidder. It was a small company with one crew, one crane, and one truck. Besides the crane operator and job site supervisor, there were three workers with chainsaws. Two stayed on the ground the whole time while one went up and down in the harness as the crane lifted him up to seventy feet in the air, so he could take the tree down in sections. It was both impressive and a little scary to watch him work. I asked the female supervisor whose brother owned the business if she had another guy with the skills to go up in the harness. She said no.

No business wants to be in a position where only one employee has the training and know-how to perform a necessary process or procedure. If that employee is out, for whatever reason, all work comes to a halt. For some businesses, at a certain stage in their development, this can't be avoided. But some businesses are responsible for keeping themselves in this precarious position.

A way to address a skills shortage and avoid the added cost of hiring another employee is to cross train the employees you already have on your payroll. The idea is to train existing employees on more than one job within the company, so you are never in the position of having no one who is able to do the work.

Here are some of the benefits of cross training:

• Every employee better understands what it takes to run the business.
• Your existing employees can cover high-demand times.
• Cross-training can reveal hidden talents of existing employees.
• It helps employees to appreciate each other's jobs.
• It gives employees the opportunity to make new relationships within the company.
• It gives you another way to provide the training and development that employees want.

FOR FURTHER REFLECTION

Developing your employees benefits your company as much as it benefits them. From increased profit to improved efficiency, products, and services, employees hold the key to your success. Their development is also your gain. Consider the following questions before moving on to *Retention Talks*.

1. What development were you given by a supervisor or company that changed your career?

2. How do you and your organization go about developing your employees?

3. What do you think of Zig Ziglar's quote, "You can have everything in life you want if you help enough other people get what they want"?

4. Are there any critical tasks in your organization where only one person has the ability or knowledge to perform? What can you do to change this?

Chapter 10

Retention Talks

W hen Jim finished the third grade, his dad and mom moved him and his older brother and sister from Columbus, Indiana, to Madison, a small town on Lake Erie in northern Ohio. This would be the first of three moves his family would make, each one because his dad, Bob Rogers, was either being promoted or taking a better job with a different company. In this case it was a promotion within Reliance Electric to be the manager of their Ashtabula, Ohio plant.

Becoming a plant manager was a pretty special moment for Mr. Rogers. He has told us the story of being a boy and sitting at the dinner table one evening with his mom and dad and brothers and sisters, and his dad, who was a factory worker, had some news. They all grew quiet and listened intently as he told of how he was working at his machine that day and the factory manager came up and had a conversation with him. Bob remembers how much this meant to his dad and the whole family; they were all so impressed. It was as if the mundane job of working at his machine all day was suddenly injected with value and importance.

How meaningful it is then that when Mr. Rogers became a plant manager, he made it a practice to walk through his plant every day and talk to the guys who ran the machines. He said he would just approach them and chat, letting them guide the conversation. I'm sure he saw his own dad in many of those men.

On one such day, he was walking through having conversations when one fella said, "We missed you yesterday, Mr. Rogers. Where were you?" He explained that he was away visiting a Reliance Electric customer. The plant worker then commented that in the twenty years he had worked there he had never visited a customer. He wasn't implying anything with that statement but sharing a thought. Well, this lingered with Mr. Rogers, and it led to an idea. He decided he would take as many of the plant workers who wanted to go, including their families, to visit Joy Manufacturing, a Reliance Electric customer located near Erie, Pennsylvania.

And that is what he did. The visit was arranged and scheduled for a Saturday, a day when the Reliance plant was closed. Originally, Mr. Rogers thought maybe thirty men from the plant might want to go. In the end, three school buses filled with close to two-hundred plant workers and some of their family members, made the one-hundred-fifty-mile round trip to visit Joy Manufacturing. The buses were procured from the local public school system because the spouse of one of the employees sat on the school board. In telling this story, Mr. Rogers describes it as the best initiative of his career.

By getting out of his office and having conversations with his employees on their turf, Jim's dad was communicating with more than just words, but with actions also. His actions said:

- Thank you for the work that you do here.
- I value you enough to spend time with you.

- I'm interested in what you have to say, and what I can learn from you.
- I want to know who you are as a person.
- You and I are in this together.
- I am available if you need anything.
- Without the work you do I wouldn't have a job.

I think my father-in-law might have been a little ahead of his time in his relational style of leadership. The old model of leadership entailed more of a transactional relationship between the manager and the employee. The employee would typically work for the company that paid the most for their labor and if the employer took something away the employee might give less in return.

In the new model of leadership, the supervisor takes an interest in the whole person who works for them, wanting to help them succeed in every area of their life, not just at work. Companies have recognized that it is in their interest to take a more holistic interest in the people who work for them. This creates relationships which then builds trust, loyalty, and more satisfied, engaged, and productive employees. It doesn't matter that companies do this to benefit themselves; what matters is that it is authentic and sincere.

When I work with leaders in group training or within one-on-one executive coaching, I encourage this more holistic approach. I acknowledge that it will require more effort from them up front, but the result will be a higher employee retention rate with a workforce that can produce more value.

If you just consider the time it takes to implement such an approach, you might not do it. You have to track time across the whole equation, not just the time you put in up front. In the end you will be able to concentrate on more important initiatives because you are spending less time recruiting, hiring, and training new employees.

THE DREAM MANAGER

Today I listen to more books than I read. My days are so full that listening is simply more practical. A recent listen was *The Dream Manager* by Matthew Kelly.

The Dream Manager is a fictitious story about a janitorial company with a 400 percent turnover rate. Something had to be done! Eventually the general manager, through trial and discovery, swerved into the idea that helping employees fulfill their dreams could build company loyalty and make them want to stay. So a position was created, a dream manager, to counsel people one-on-one to help make their dreams a reality.

You're probably thinking, *Yeah, that's fine for a fictional company, but that will never happen in real life.* I get that; the story is a bit far-fetched in that you're unlikely to ever create a position strictly to manage employee's dreams. And yet, I agree with the author Matthew Kelly, this is the type of unorthodox thinking that is required to attract and retain more of your employees. If one of my past supervisors had sat down with me and asked to know my dreams, and then acted to help make them a reality, I am certain my sense of loyalty to the company would have grown, giving me more reasons to stay with them.

THE BEST RETENTION TOOL I KNOW

Your employees come into your organization having one of four mindsets. And the quality of their experience in the *Employee Engagement Environment* determines whether they have remained in that mindset or whether their mindset has changed. Remember that they are evaluating everything, but you can't see what they are thinking. Without a mechanism to bring their thoughts to light, you're left guessing what their mindset might be, and so you might be caught off guard when a top performer decides to leave. Your goal is to move your employees ever higher through the four mindsets until they think of you as a *Career Company*. To have more success doing this, it helps greatly to know what employees are thinking, and there is no better tool for this than what I call *Retention Talks*.

A *Retention Talk* is a scheduled face-to-face conversation between a supervisor and one of his or her employees where the supervisor asks questions, listens to the employee's responses, and answers any questions the employee may have. This is not a performance evaluation nor is it a skills or knowledge test. This is a time carved out especially for the employee that reflects the same sentiments Bob Rogers did when he talked with the guys in the plant.

- Thank you for the work that you do here.
- I value you enough to spend time with you.
- I'm interested in what you have to say and what I can learn from you.
- I want to know who you are as a person.
- You and I are in this together.
- I am available if you need anything.
- Without the work you do I wouldn't have a job.

While those sentiments capture the spirit of a

successful retention talk, there are specific things we want to address and accomplish:

- To hear from the employee to discern what you as a supervisor and representative of the company can do to make their job a better work experience for them.
- To build a relationship based on trust and reap all the benefits of such a relationship like open and honest communication.
- To discover the employee's true passions, so you can develop and train them in areas that interest them.
- To merge the interests of the employee with the interests of the company for a mutually beneficial relationship.
- To learn of any pertinent information about the employee's future with the company so you have the opportunity to address it.

THE EMPLOYEE ENGAGEMENT SHORTFALL

Just like companies put their best foot forward in their mission and marketing statements, they do something similar when they interview new job applicants. They have a standard for what it should be like to work for their company. I call it the *Employee Engagement Ideal*. This ideal is what they often present to potential job applicants as a means to convince them to come work for their company. But because this ideal represents the very best they have to offer an employee, it is almost inevitable that they will come up short to some degree. I call this the *Employee Engagement Shortfall*. Another purpose for *Retention Talks* is to hear from employees as to how you are doing in delivering the work experience that was presented and promised to them in the interview. This then helps you measure the degree of your *Employee Engagement Shortfall*.

THE SCRIPT

A *Retention Talk* is only going to be as good as the one conducting it. To set the right tone, think of the talk as if you are sitting down with a friend to have a meaningful conversation. This will serve to take away some of the hierarchy that naturally exists within the supervisor-employee relationship and will place you on more equal footing, which will encourage openness and honesty. To reinforce this, I recommend that supervisors have this conversation somewhere other than their office.

Having prepared and pre-selected questions will help you stay on point and accomplish your purpose for the talk. There is a quote by Henry David Thoreau which can serve as a reminder for what to do once you have asked your question. "The greatest compliment that was ever paid me was when one asked me what I thought, and attended to my answer." By listening attentively, the employee will sense your sincere interest in their answer and be more willing to elaborate. This will also let you know what unscripted questions to then ask as a follow up to get more details and clarity. Let the natural exchange of conversation take place until you've exhausted a subject and then move on to the next question.

The number of scripted questions is only limited by your imagination, but there are certain topics you want to make sure your questions address. Here are some possible questions you can ask:

- Are we giving you everything you need to do your job well?
- Is there anything I am doing as your supervisor that is holding you back?
- Is there anything I am doing as your supervisor that is helping you that you want me to keep doing?
- What do you most enjoy about your job?
- What do you least like about your job?
- Is there a specific training you desire?

In my *Retention Talk* training, I recommend that supervisors sit down two-to-four times each year to have these conversations. You want to keep a file of their noteworthy answers along with any promises or actions you committed to taking. But this notetaking is better done on your own after you have had the conversation. This allows you to give them your undivided attention during the talk itself. If a topic is addressed with important details, and you feel it needs to be written down right away so you can accurately remember it, then make that exception.

Like any powerful tool, *Retention Talks* must be used responsibly. Used irresponsibly, they can hurt you. For instance, if you don't follow through and do what you promised, the integrity of the whole process is compromised. Here are some more tips from the retention talk safety manual:

- Do not turn it into a performance evaluation.

• Do not be argumentative or use your power against them.

• Make sure to protect the employee's privacy by keeping certain things confidential. When in doubt, err on the side of not saying anything. Ask if they mind you sharing with others in the company anything they have said.

• Do not ask them to gossip or tell on their fellow employees. Tell them up front that you don't want to hear anything of the sort.

DETERMINING RETENTION STATUS

The mindsets of *Insignificant, Temporary, Exclusive,* and *Career Company* reflect the level of commitment employees have about your organization. By asking certain questions in the *Retention Talks*, along with observing their overall demeanor throughout the conversation, you should be able to identify each employee's mindset with some accuracy. This can give you a picture of what your retention rate might look like over the next six months; help you prepare for possible vacancies in key positions based upon what you hear; and give you time to address grievances before they ever decide to leave. Here are a couple questions you could ask to help reveal mindset:

• Have you thought of leaving our company in the last six months to one year? If so, why?
• Do you see yourself still working here two years from now? One year?

THE PERFECT RETENTION TALK

In one of my training sessions, James, one of the twelve leaders in the room, shared the success he had in having a *Retention Talk* with one of his team members. The talk was with an experienced technician who was paid piece rate, meaning his pay was determined by how much he produced. His production level was hit or miss, having some good weeks, and some not so good. On average his output was low, equal to what you might expect to see from an employee who was working a twenty-five- to thirty-hour week. This was far below his potential plus it was setting a bad example for the other technicians.

James met with him and asked the right questions. How are things going? I know you would like to produce more because that would increase your pay. What can I do to help? James did not turn the *Retention Talk* into a performance evaluation. He did not assume anything negative about the situation. The technician had a supervisor who was saying in so many words, I want to help you be your best!

The trust this established made the employee comfortable enough to admit that he struggled with organization, keeping his area clean, and staying on task. So they created a plan to meet every morning for fifteen minutes to set his progress for that day based on what was on the schedule. Their plan included two additional touch points later in the day, so James could track and encourage his progress.

The technician's average weekly output jumped to what you would expect to see from an employee working a fifty- to fifty-five-hour week, almost double his previous level. Extrapolating that production level over a one-year period, James figured it would bring in an additional hundred thousand for the company. But it gets even better. James supervises nineteen technicians. Think of the added income if they all increased their production output.

FOR FURTHER REFLECTION

A *Retention Talk* is a time for you to get to know your employees' goals and mindset about their position, the company, and how you can help them grow. Consider these points carefully and then start scheduling your talks.

1. What are the benefits of supervisors really getting to know their people?

2. Have any of your past supervisors ever had *Retention Talks* with you? If so, did it change the way you viewed the supervisor or the company itself?

3. What part of the *Retention Talk* agrees or disagrees with you?

4. Who are you going to have a *Retention Talk* with?

Chapter 11

Conflict Management

W hen I talk about conflict in the workplace, it is not with the misconception that we can eliminate it. At a press conference following the Los Angeles riots in 1992, Rodney King famously asked, "Can we all get along?" The answer is most can, but not all. The human race has never known peace. In the book of Genesis we read that a murder was committed in the very first family, when Cain killed his brother Abel. Every recorded war in history after that is a conflict that couldn't be resolved by peaceful means.

I will leave it to the theologians and philosophers to tell us why all men cannot get along. But whatever you attribute it to, wherever men, women, and children gather, there you will find conflict. And of course, this conflict also occurs in our places of work.

So, if it is not to eliminate what cannot be eliminated, then what do we do about the conflict in our companies and organizations? For one, we don't ignore it. Unresolved conflict will give some of your employees a reason to leave, especially if that conflict exists between them and their supervisor. Each one of your employees has a mindset that is fluid, free to flow in any direction between *Insignificant*, *Temporary*, *Exclusive*, and *Career Company*. Your goal is to

147

accomplish the harder thing of moving them up, ever closer to a *Career Company* mindset. Unresolved conflict, however, will move them down the path of least resistance to where they see you as *Temporary* or *Insignificant*. When that happens, it is only a matter of time before they leave, and you incur the high costs of replacing them.

It is no wonder that they would want to leave if nothing is done about it. Conflict often makes us feel unmotivated and distracted, angry, frustrated, nervous, and anxious. These are feelings most people want to avoid. It is this avoidance that results in more cases of employee sickness and absence from work. But avoiding conflict does nothing to remove it, leaving issues unresolved and free to cause more damage.

In fact, unresolved conflict is cancerous. It can spread, consuming more and more of the persons directly involved until they see everything else through the filter of the conflict to the point that it impairs their perception and judgement. The conflict can also spread to those persons not directly involved but standing nearby. These bystanders might be asked or even feel obligated to take sides. This is especially damaging when it involves people in senior-level positions. Once people take sides, they begin to feel the need to justify their position by their words and actions, causing further division.

A swift resolution to conflict, therefore, is good for the health of the organization. Get it early and get it all is what I say. Anything left behind will live below the surface only to become a problem at some time in the future.

What you want to do is manage conflict to prevent

it where you can, address and resolve it as quickly as you can. Limit its negative effects by preventing its spread and using it to your advantage where you can. But not just the conflict within your company, you also want to manage the conflict between you and your customers and clients. Your business can't survive if it always has to generate new clients and customers for sales to replace those who have left. It is challenging to get new customers and clients, so you want to nurture and protect the relationships you have and one way you do that is through effective conflict management.

Some of the costs of conflict are:

- The loss of valued employees.
- The cost to replace employees who have left because of unresolved conflict.
- The drain on HR resources.
- The drop in employee productivity because employees avoid conflict causing sickness and absence from work.
- The drop in employee productivity because employees are distracted by conflict.
- The loss of customers and clients.
- The cost of finding new customers and clients.

CAUSES OF CONFLICT

Differences in personality are one of conflict's major causes. In every situation there are the facts of the matter and the conclusions that people then draw from those facts. But in between the facts and the conclusions is the person, meaning their unique experiences and memories, their personal preferences and biases, their passions, and their personality type. Facts have to filter through all of that before we ever arrive at our conclusions, and these greatly affect how we see the world. This explains why two different people can draw entirely different conclusions from the same set of facts setting up the possibility of conflict.

Overworked and stressed out employees are another major cause of conflict. When the dominant mindset of your employees is *Insignificant* or *Temporary*, one of the symptoms is you won't always have enough people to do the work. Employees are constantly being asked to work longer and harder, which creates a very stressful work environment. Conflict is a natural byproduct of such an environment.

Poor leadership ranks high among the causes of conflict. John Maxwell says everything rises and falls with leadership, and it is certainly true about conflict. The supervisor has the power to make conflict resolution a priority and address it. They are in the position to be a positive role model for resolving conduct and how to have conversations that do just that.

One of the most effective ways for supervisors to discover and address conflict is through one-on-one *Retention Talks* and other more informal conversations with each employee. In this way they can stay connected to what is happening among their team members.

Much of the conflict occurs at the entry-level and front-line positions. This is where it is critical that supervisors be able to act as a mediator to help team members resolve their conflicts. They can also counsel individual employees on how to best deal with a dispute they might find themselves in.

Some of the major causes of conflict:

- Personality differences
- Overworked employees
- Stress
- Poor leadership
- Lack of honesty and openness
- Roles not clearly defined by management
- Lack of accountability
- Value differences
- Shortage of resources

Conflict can lead to:

- Personal insults and attacks as emotions run high
- Work absence and sick days
- Project failure
- Cross departmental conflict
- Bullying
- Higher turnover as people leave or are fired
- People have to be moved to different departments

What supervisors can do to manage conflict:

- Have *Retention Talks.*
- Act as a mediator.
- Clearly define roles.
- Pair people together who complement one another.
- Continually talk about the importance of managing conflict.
- Pay special attention to the person who is toxic and be ready to remove them.

- Be a role model for how to work well with others.
- Provide conflict resolution training.

CONFLICT RESOLUTION TRAINING

Companies benefit when they make conflict resolution a priority of the organization and train for it. The training acts as a lifeline that provides the means for people to pull themselves back together. It is most effective when the whole organization is trained to be on the conflict resolution team. Much like you continually marinate the organization in its mission, continue to explain the importance of conflict resolution between all employees on all levels. This will provide understanding that will motivate everyone to be part of the solution.

The training is designed to enable employees to look for and create solutions where both sides are pleased with the outcome, a win-win. Win-win solutions, when possible, are superior to win-lose solutions. Win-lose solutions can permanently resolve a conflict. The person on the losing side may learn that what they did will never work, so they move on and leave it behind. But a win-lose scenario can result in bitter feelings that never truly resolve the conflict. Like the villain in a horror movie, it never dies.

Conflict resolution training gives people the confidence to attempt to resolve their conflict rather than avoid it. They believe they can actually do it and succeed rather than make the situation worse. Their confidence creates success which creates more confidence. They develop a *Confidence of Competence* when it comes to conflict resolution.

TOUGH TALKS

Conflict is resolved when the people directly involved get inside a room and talk it out. I call these *Tough Talks*. Notice I didn't say tough text messages or tough emails. Writing a note expressing an apology or an explanation can be a good start, but it does not take the place of face-to-face contact. The written word is limited because it includes the "what we say" but not the "how we say it." Without the body language, eye contact, and inflections of the voice, there is the potential to create more misunderstanding and make the situation even worse.

Left to our own devices, the conversations we have to address differences of opinion often become unruly power struggles. If it helps, just imagine a professional football game played between two teams without referees, where each side is left to manage its conduct. It might start out with the best of intentions but soon one team will cross the line then the other feels compelled to respond in kind, and the game eventually spirals out of control.

Training for *Tough Talks* provides a set of techniques and rules you can follow so that the conversation can be played fairly, where each side can fully have its say, where all the facts and the conclusions that have been drawn can be discussed with respect and seriously considered. The end goal is to create a win-win solution for each person involved, accompanied by any future actions of who does what by when, so that the conflict is fully resolved or on track to be resolved.

CONFLICT BENEFITS

Conflict is a reality that does have its benefits. If two people are both committed to creating something great, but they differ on how to get there, there could be conflict. But if this conflict lives more like a friendly competition, it can be positive. Treated this way, they can actually push each other to greater heights, exposing the weaknesses and strengths of the other person's point of view, ultimately creating something superior than had they created it alone. They might even create something truly innovative.

If supervisors can hold their teams together by managing conflict, they will enjoy the benefits of superior decision-making by a group. It starts with putting the right people together on the team. Putting the wrong personalities together on a team is a way of asking for conflict. Therefore, it is important to get to know the personalities of your team members to group people together who complement one another. Letting team members have a say in this can be helpful in accomplishing this. That is not to say we want total harmony. It is proven that a diversity of opinion creates superior decision making and avoids groupthink.

Finally, conflict can be the price we pay for greater intimacy which improves our working relationships. We learn a lot about another person when we are in conflict with them. Do they play fair, do they play by any rules at all, can they see your point of view, do they listen? All of this leads to a better understanding of one another. We won't always like what we see, either in them or in ourselves, but this provides a mirror for us to identify areas we can grow.

Whether we are talking about conflict within your own organization or conflict with your customers and clients, I invite the companies and supervisors I train to view conflict as an opportunity. By handling it honestly and directly, you can actually build trusting and loyal relationships because everyone will know that when the inevitable conflict arises in the future, you are a faithful partner they can trust to work through it.

FOR FURTHER REFLECTION

Conflict is inevitable in organizational settings. Therefore, training for and addressing conflict in a positive manner helps build relationships and trust that ultimately increases employee loyalty. Below are questions to help you assess and begin to address conflict within your company.

1. Are you prone to avoid conflict or face it head on?

2. To what degree should supervisors get involved in the conflicts between team members?

3. Do you have a technique for resolving conflict or do you handle each situation differently?

4. Describe a situation where you successfully resolved an issue with another person. What was the key to your success?

5. How does unresolved conflict hurt an organization?

Chapter 12

HR Practices

T he fifth part of the *Retention Architecture* is HR practices that keep us out of court and take us into the future. We have included several chapters on what is important to find, retain, and engage talent. This chapter is the stuff not mentioned. The stuff employees want from their employer and the stuff needed to keep our business running and out of court.

Firstly, every organization that is fortunate enough to have a full time HR professional will hopefully have government regulations and legal compliance requirements in place. As I work with smaller to midsize companies, they don't always have this luxury. They might have an HR manager that is newer and has some experience and could use some help from either a HR consultant or employment law attorney. Or an HR manager who understands that bringing in a consultant from the outside to train and help implement new programs will not only enhance the organizational effectiveness but the overall culture.

As an HR consultant firm, our team offers services that will assess current practices and assist with implementation. Why? Because no matter how successful you have been with the other four parts of the *Retention Architecture*, without government regulations and legal compliance, you could be forced to close your doors.

As an HR professional involved in my local Society of Human Resources Management (SHRM) chapter (Big Bend SHRM), and the HR Florida State Council I have had the opportunity to meet and work with some HR pros. I have also had the opportunity to work with some great employment law attorneys and partner with them to train on how to stay out of court. One attorney and friend shared a story of taking on a client after they were in trouble. The client owned ten barber shops in Florida's panhandle where I live. The family-owned business filed for bankruptcy and locked its doors over a legal dispute over whether the stylists were independent contractors or regular employees.

They were hit with two separate federal lawsuits by four barbers claiming they were misclassified as independent contractors. There was no way the family-owned business could pay an attorney to defend them against this lawsuit. Even if they won the suit, the owners would have to pay their own legal expenses out of pocket. And they still faced the Equal Employment Opportunity Commission (EEOC) complaints and other possible federal action.

This is one of hundreds of stories I have heard over the years. One of the reasons I went into HR is to help my employer stay out of court. Now I help many employers do the same.

Some of the questions an organization wants to ask themselves are:

1. Are positions correctly classified? Exempt, nonexempt, employee or independent contractor?

2. Is the handbook up to date?

3. Are job descriptions current for all positions?

4. Is new hire vetting done in a legal order? What is the employment law process?

5. How are hours tracked?

6. What benefit plans are offered? Who handles COBRA administration for the organization?

7. Are discipline and termination matters handled properly? Are managers trained in this area?

8. What is the turnover rate for the organization? What is the cost?

When we are hired by a company, we perform an organizational audit. As mentioned, before we look at the talent acquisition program, survey employees to find out more about leadership, development, conflict resolution, and of course HR practices. Some of the things we will look for and offer are:

- Turnover Rate and Cost Analysis
- Discipline and Termination Practices
- Safety: Accident Reporting (Worker Compensation/OSHA)
- Performance Evaluation Process
- Employment Offer (Contingent or non-contingent)

- Employment Application Forms
- Interview and Hiring Procedures
- Job Description Development or Review
- New-Hire Onboarding Practices
- Benefit Plans Administration – Review and COBRA Process
- Policy Development & Administration
- I-9 and E-Verify Compliance
- Personnel Files Handling (location, protected information separation)
- Employee Handbook Development or Review
- Employee Relations Guidance
- Proper Personnel Classification (exempt versus nonexempt)
- Time and Attendance Practices and Records
- Payroll Processing
- HRIS/Payroll System
- Tax Obligations and Mandatory Reporting including the Affordable Care Act (ACA)
- HR Staff Structure and Placement

The second part of HR practices is how must HR lead us into the new competitive workplace. Our President of SHRM, Johnny C. Taylor, Jr. says that "We need people." He called the hot economy, a slowed birthrate and a still unsorted worker immigration situation "the perfect storm" — and the perfect reason to focus on untapped talent pools. CEOs, Taylor noted, want their HR departments to keep them out of trouble. But finding talent is a close second priority. "Two years ago we were talking about avoiding age discrimination lawsuits," Taylor said "Now, we are telling HR people how to hire older workers."

As employees continue to be in the driver's seat, meaning many of them have more than one offer, what is it that they are looking for in an organization to attract, hire, and retain them?

In a highly competitive marketplace, companies need to make sure they are offering more than just competitive pay and benefits to attract the best workers. Fair salaries and medical benefits are no longer enough to attract workers to a new organization. It all comes down to offering certain perks and benefits that truly resonate with the worker of today. Now as much as it pains me to say this, it comes with a great economy and more opportunities not only for the employee but for business also.

If you think about it…all employees, regardless of age, want the same thing, the same thing we want ourselves. I am not a Millennial, but the list below is what I wanted in a job, and these are the same they want. Here are a few things companies need to address as we move forward.

- Blend of Work/Life
- Permanent Flexibility
- Culture—Leadership and Conflict Resolution
- Talent Development—Coaching, Mentoring, Performance Plans, Cross Training, Job Shadowing, Job Enlargement, Enrichment, Job Rotation
- Compensation and Benefits

BALANCING THE WORK/LIFE

Today's employees, no matter what generation, are seeking fulfillment across their work and personal lives. The fast pace of life in which we lead can leave people feeling overwhelmed or like they are falling short in one or both areas.

Organizations now more than ever, recognize the need for flexibility and support of workers not only in the workplace but both in the lives of their people personally.

Employees often state that one of their biggest sources of stress is personal finances. Regardless of age, finances keep us all up at night. Can I afford to retire? Will I outlive my retirement? Do I have enough savings if I couldn't work? Will my family be taken care of if I were gone?

One of my clients offers his employees time to meet with a financial planner that comes to the workplace and helps employees assess their retirement. I believe this is a huge piece of mind for employees and benefits many don't consider.

FLEXIBILITY

One of the reasons we see such an increase in the gig economy now is that full-time workers want more flexibility. They seek:

- Flexible schedule
- Ability to work where they want
- Ability to take on multiple different projects

"The 2018 Global Talent Trends" study by Mercer collected input from eight hundred business executives and eighteen hundred HR leaders, as well as more than five thousand employees across twenty-one industries and forty-four countries around the world. The study identified top talent trends, which can be useful for companies who are trying to stay ahead of the game when it comes to employee satisfaction.

Among the findings, Mercer identified permanent workplace flexibility as one of the top interest of employees and applicants.

It's clear that the strict nine-to-five workday is outdated, and it won't help employers attract or maintain today's top talent. The study found that 51 percent of employees wish their company offered more flexible work options. No matter the industry, flexibility is incredibly important to employees and job seekers across the nation. Companies that offer employees flexibility in the form of telecommuting, flexible schedules and unlimited PTO help employees maintain a positive work-life balance. Flexibility has also been shown to reduce workplace stress, boost mental well-being and encourage productivity."

ALL ABOUT THE CULTURE

If we were to believe the media, we would think that our talent wants ping pong tables, a huge slide in the foyer, 'round-the-clock activities, and gourmet meals. All of this sounds cool, but it is a fad. This forces us to keep up with "What's next?"

Gallup has reported for years that over two-thirds of employees are disengaged at work, which leads to poor performance, morale, productivity, and profits.

In order to change this statistic, we must change with the times. We can embrace AI, the gig economy, and permanent flexibility—or we can be left behind. But regardless of how fast an organization can move forward, one thing will always remain, employees seek a culture where they have some autonomy, great relationships, meaningful work and fair pay, and benefits. Culture, how people are treated, respected, developed, and cared for will always trump the next fad in any workplace.

FOR FURTHER REFLECTION

HR best practices encompass every facet of an employee's relationship with the company they work for. And because employees are your most valuable asset, attention to HR practices is crucial to your organizations continued success and growth. Consider these questions related to your current HR practices, and consider what improvements can be implemented.

1. What has your company done to meet the needs of the new generation of employees?

2. What changes do you need to make to improve the workplace for the new generation you are leading?

3. How is your company culture?

Conclusion

The natural state of things is disorder. Sustained human effort is required to impose order, otherwise, a state of disorder will remain. Left to its own devices, anyone's yard will be a weed infested mess. There are degrees of imposed order and each person decides for themselves how nice of a yard they want to have, and how much effort they are willing to exert to have it. They decide how important it is compared to all the other things they want to do in life.

This pertains to every human activity that requires thought, including starting and maintaining a company. The moment the idea for a business is conceived, the move from disorder to order commences: the viability of the idea is considered in the mind or minds of the person or persons who conceived of it; discussions take place about its chances for success and what would be required to make the business a reality; the money needed to invest and build the business is obtained; all requirements to satisfy regulations, permits and licenses are met; a building or office space or online infrastructure from which to do business is found or built; service equipment and inventory is purchased; employees are hired; and the doors are opened for business.

A business then commits to the long process of establishing itself and becoming ever more successful.

What typically happens is at a point determined by the drive, determination, and skill of its leaders, a business will attain and settle at a level of success that leadership deems acceptable. This is where the company says we could probably improve, but we can live with this. I call this *the Livable Plateau.* If everything basically stays the same, the company will remain on this plateau until someone or something comes along to propel them to move higher. Until that happens, a company will live at a certain level of:

- Talent
- Turnover
- Leadership
- Trust
- Communication
- Conflict

If you want to succeed in business, then find out what the most successful businesses are doing and copy them. One thing you will find is that the most successful do not reside on *the Livable Plateau.* They are always reaching for higher ground by addressing inefficiencies and creating better systems. When you are operating at peak performance levels it becomes very difficult to find ways to climb higher, but that upward drive is the very thing that allows you to sustain those peak performance levels and not drop any lower.

Retention Architecture can be the propeller that moves your company off of *the Livable Plateau.* Some people say to me, "Colene, I see the need to strengthen the *Retention Architecture* of my business, but I just don't have time, it is all we can do to meet the daily demands of our business." In return I say, "I get that!" The *Retention Architecture* is a time saving, time creating initiative. Once strengthened, you will be free of the frustrations of high turnover, and you will have more time to do those things you have always wanted to do for your business.

Endnotes

1. Bob Rodgers, The Hidden Costs of Employee Turnover, HR Magazine, 27.

2. "Medium," How Much Does Employee Turnover Really Cost?, assessed 3/10/2020,

3. https://medium.com/resources-for-humans/how-much-does-employee-turnover-really-cost-d61df5eed151.

4. "HR Dive," The Hidden Costs of Turnover, accessed 3/10/2020, https://www.hrdive.com/news/shrm-ceo-hr-faces-a-perfect-storm-and-the-perfect-opportunity/557633/.

5. "Medium," How Much Does Employee Turnover Really Cost?, assessed 3/10/2020,

6. https://medium.com/resources-for-humans/how-much-does-employee-turnover-really-cost-d61df5eed151.

7. "CDC," History of the Surgeon General's Reports on Smoking and Health, accessed 3/10/2020, https://www.cdc.gov/tobacco/data_statistics/sgr/history/index.htm.

8. "Medium," How Much Does Employee Turnover Really Cost?, assessed 3/10/2020,

9. https://medium.com/resources-for-humans/how-much-does-employee-turnover-really-cost-d61df5eed.

10. "SHRM News," "4 Things to Know about Employees with a Criminal History," accessed March 10, 2020, https://hrindianashrm.org/news/4-things-to-know-about-employees-with-a

11. "Learn G2," Onboarding Statistics, accessed 3/10/2020, https://learn.g2.com/onboarding-statistics.

12. "SHRM," Onboarding Key Retaining Engaging Talent, https://www.shrm.org/resourcesandtools/hr-topics/talent-acquisition/pages/onboarding-key-retaining-engaging-talent.aspx.

13. "SHRM News," Don't Underestimate the Importance of Effec-

tive Onboarding, accessed 3/10/2020, https://www.shrm.org/resourcesandtools/hr-topics/talent-acquisition/pages/dont-under-estimate-the-importance-of-effective-onboarding.aspx.

14. Maxwell, John, The 21 Irrefutable Laws of Leadership, (Nashville: Thomas Nelson, 1998), 13.

15. "Brainy Quote," Margaret Thatcher, accessed 3/10/2020, https://www.brainyquote.com/quotes/margaret_thatcher_109592.

16. "Proverb Hunter," Proverb Hunter, accessed 3/10/2020, http://proverbhunter.com/quote/he-that-thinketh-he-leadeth-and-hath-no-one-following-him-is-only-taking-a-walk/.

17. "View from the Top," John Maxwell on How to Lead Yourself, accessed 3/10/2020, https://www.viewfromthetop.com/blog/john-maxwell-on-how-to-lead-yourself.

18. Kelly, Matthew, The Dream Manager, (New York: Beacon Publishing, 2007), 124.

19. Kelly, Matthew, The Dream Manager, (New York: Beacon Publishing, 2007), 63.

20. The Art of Improvement, 7 Crucial Lessons People Often Learn Too Late In Life, YouTube Video 6:02, Streamed Live April 14, 2019, https://www.youtube.com/watch?v=WbvdOuo9pkc.

21. "Winston Churchill," The Battle of Britain Excerpt of the Best Little Stories of Winston Churchill, Accessed 3/10/2020, https://winstonchurchill.org/publications/churchill-bulletin/bulletin-040-oct-2011/the-battle-of-britainexcerpt-of-qthe-best-little-stories-of-winston-churchillq-by-c-brian-kelly/.

22. Braveheart, Directed by Mel Gibson. Performed by Mel Gibson, Produced by Icon Production and The Ladd Company, Distributed by Paramount Pictures.

23. "Church Bulletin," The Battle of Britain Excerpt of the Best Little Stories of Winston Churchill, accessed 3/10/2020, https://winstonchurchill.org/publications/churchill-bulletin/bulletin-040-oct-2011/the-battle-of-britainexcerpt-of-qthe-best-little-stories-of-winston-churchillq-by-c-brian-kelly/.

24. Ibid.

25. "Art of Manliness," Lessons in Manliness, Benjamin Franklin's Pursuit of the Virtuous Life, accessed 3/10/2020, https://www.artofmanliness.com/articles/lessons-in-manliness-benjamin-franklins-pursuit-of-the-virtuous-life/.

26. Miller, Donald, Building a Storybrand, (Nashville: HarperCollins Leadership, 2017).

27. "ABC News," Tom Hanks Portrays Mister Rogers Beautiful Day Neighborhood, accessed 3/10/2020.

28. https://abcnews.go.com/Entertainment/tom-hanks-portrays-mister-rogers-beautiful-day-neighborhood/story?id=67149941.

29. Capra, Frank, Frances Goodrich, Albert Hackett, Jo Swerling, James Stewart, Donna Reed, Lionel Barrymore, et al. 1998. Frank Capra's it's a wonderful life. [United States]: Republic Entertainment.

30. "Beliefnet," A Loving Person Lives in a Hostile World," accessed 3/10/2020, https://www.beliefnet.com/quotes/inspiration/k/ken-keyes-jr/a-loving-person-lives-in-a-loving-world-a-hostile.aspx.

31. Ibid.

32. "The Week," Feeling Pain, accessed 3/10/2020, https://theweek.com/articles/471681/feeling-pain.

33. Ibid.

34. "Brainy Quote," Theodore Roosevelt, accessed 3/10/2020, https://www.brainyquote.com/quotes/theodore_roosevelt_140484.

35. "Grossmont," Instructional Resources, Study Aids all the Good Things, accessed 3/10/2020

36. https://www.grossmont.edu/people/karl-sherlock/english-098/instructional-resources/study-aid-all-the-good-things.aspx.

37. "Goodreads," You Can Have Everything in Life You Want if You, accessed 3/10/2020,

38. https://www.goodreads.com/quotes/1177933-you-can-have-ev-

erything-in-life-you-want-if-you.

39. "Brainy Quote," Robert Baden Powell, accessed 3/10/2020,

40. https://www.brainyquote.com/quotes/robert_badenpow-
    ell_753084.

41. Kelly, Matthew, The Dream Manager, (New York: Beacon Pub-
    lishing), 2007.

42. "Goodreads," Quotable Quotes, accessed 3/10/2020,

43. https://www.goodreads.com/quotes/62259-the-greatest-compli-
    ment-that-was-ever-paid-me-was-when.

44. "Shmoop," Press Conference: Can We All Get Along?, accessed
    3/10/2020, https://www.shmoop.com/quotes/can-we-all-get-
    along.html.

45. "HR Dive," SHRM CEO Faces a Perfect Storm and the Perfect
    Opportunity, accessed 3/10/2020,

46. https://www.hrdive.com/news/shrm-ceo-hr-faces-a-perfect-
    storm-and-the-perfect-opportunity/557633/.

47. "HR Dive," Finding the Right Talent Is 2019s Top Pain, ac-
    cessed 3/10/2020, https://www.hrdive.com/news/finding-the-
    right-talent-is-2019s-top-pain-point-for-ceos/550474/.

48. "HR Dive," SHRM CEO Faces a Perfect Storm and the Perfect
    Opportunity, accessed 3/10/2020,

49. https://www.hrdive.com/news/shrm-ceo-hr-faces-a-perfect-
    storm-and-the-perfect-opportunity/557633/.

50. "Mercer," Global talent Trends Study 2018, accessed 3/10/2020,
    https://www.asean.mercer.com/newsroom/global-talent-trends-
    study-2018.html.

51. "Gallup," Employee Engagement Rise, accessed 3/10/2020,

52. https://news.gallup.com/poll/241649/employee-engagement-rise.
    aspx.

Learn How You Can Work with Colene

"My mission is to relieve companies of the excessive costs and frustrations associated with high turnover by increasing their retention rate through leadership development, talent development, and conflict management. This creates a more engaging, productive and profitable environment that motivates employees to stay."

KEYNOTE SPEAKER

Retention isn't just another issue; it is the issue companies face today. From her 25-year background in HR and sales, Colene's expertise provides solutions that retain top talent. She engages audiences  through her unique expert insights and real-world client stories that add authenticity to the learning.

COLENE'S KEYNOTE PRESENTATIONS

Employee Solutions: How to get them, how to keep them.

Whether there are more jobs than people to fill them or fewer jobs than potential candidates, leaders cite recruiting and retention as their biggest challenge. In every job economy, losing your best people impacts productivity, disrupts leadership, and reduces morale, which all equal a huge cost to the company. One person can't tackle this problem alone; it has to be a company-wide initiative. In this presentation, solutions are provided that are both repeatable and sustainable, designed to improve your employee's work experience so that they continually say "I want to work here."

The Future of HR: Strategic partnerships that create acquisition, engagement, and retention solutions.

More than ever before, organizations are looking to HR to help solve the employee retention issue that is the challenge of every company. HR is well positioned to lead this effort by initiating a strategic partnership between the C-Suite, the supervisors, and themselves to create a comprehensive and coordinated turnover prevention strategy that never loses sight of delivering an engaging and positive work experience to each and every employee. The result is a more experienced, effective, and efficient workforce that leads to greater innovation and profits.

Book Colene at: www.ColeneRogers.com

*As a popular HR speaker for the Society of Human Resource Management (SHRM), Colene presents HRCI BUSINESS certified Keynotes and Workshops at SHRM state conferences

LEADERSHIP TRAINING

Leadership is a learnable skill. Colene works with leaders of every level, from the recently promoted to seasoned leaders, to gain a deeper knowledge and understanding of their leadership potential so as to increase their influence and lead their teams and themselves to greater success. Over a customizable time frame from 6 months to 1 year, Colene works with participants to set powerful goals and, more importantly, to accomplish them. This training is facilitated by using this book as a basis of discussion, reflection, and action. Colene gives participants simple assignments to enhance growth, group feedback, and application for future outcomes.

To hire Colene go to www.ColeneRogers.com

LEADERSHIP TEAM BUILDING

Based on the
leadership principles
of John Maxwell,
Colene conducts a
3-hour team building
exercise that benefits
any group of people
working toward a
common goal. Both

fun and interactive, players identify individual and
organizational strengths and weaknesses, access
communication, affirm their peers, and address difficult
topics. Organizations and teams enjoy the atmosphere
of discussion, learning, and edifying each other in a
way that is productive, strategic, and goal driven.

To hire Colene go to www.ColeneRogers.com

EXECUTIVE COACHING

Every organization's
success depends on
the effectiveness of
its leaders. As a John
Maxwell certified
coach, Colene has
been trained to take
leaders to higher levels
of leadership.

Over a customizable time frame, Colene meets

one-on-one with leaders and emerging leaders for coaching sessions on personal and professional growth, supported by powerful goal setting and accountability. Leaders come away equipped to overcome limiting self-beliefs and to lead themselves and their direct reports to greater levels of success and influence.

Coach with Colene at: www.ColeneRogers.com

CONFLICT MANAGEMENT

Conflict is inevitable. It is what we do with it that matters. Over a customizable time frame, Colene works within organizations to help them better manage conflict and limit its presence and spread. As a certified Crucial Conversations trainer, Colene teaches others the skills used by top performers to resolve conflict and achieve alignment and agreement on important matters. Individuals, teams, and entire organizations learn how to dissect the issue, recognize their role in the matter, share their interpretation of events in a non-threatening way, and to value others' perspectives. By overcoming adversity and resolving conflict, relationships are preserved and strengthened. The result is a culture characterized by trust and teamwork that results in superior decision making and efficiency.

Book Colene at: www.ColeneRogers.com

COLENE'S 90 MINUTE/HALF DAY/FULL DAY SEMINARS/ WORKSHOPS

Tough Talk Training: Conversations That Resolve Conflict and Increase Retention

There is considerable research to suggest that an organization's success is greatly affected by the way their people handle conversations where there is an issue to be resolved. Colene calls them *tough talks*. The organizational costs of avoiding these conversations or having them poorly can include:

1. Loss of clients or potential business
2. Damage to company reputation
3. High employee turnover
4. Loss of morale
5. Decreased productivity & engagement

Naturally, these amount to lost profits while opening the door to potential employment lawsuits.

In this highly interactive workshop, Colene Rogers, SHRM-SCP, a conflict resolution expert, teaches participants skills to resolve conflict where both parties can be satisfied with the outcome. This preserves and strengthens relationships and builds trust within the organization. With the use of video scenarios, stories, role playing, and more, participants leave with steps they can implement right away to have the tough talks in their life with more confidence and hope for success.

Book Colene at: www.ColeneRogers.com

RETENTION: KEY MINDSETS THAT RETAIN TOP TALENT

With retention being the goal of organizations, it is important companies recognize that no single department can solve the employee retention issue on its own. Retention requires a coordinated strategic alliance between the C-Suite, supervisors, and all departments to develop a comprehensive turnover prevention strategy that strengthens talent acquisition, effective leadership, conflict management, and talent development. This coordinated effort immunizes top talent from leaving by creating a more engaging and productive work environment resulting in higher organizational retention rates.

In this highly interactive workshop based on the material in this book (Retention: Key Mindsets That Retain Top Talent), Colene presents what she calls Retention Architecture. This architecture is what makes higher employee retention rates possible.

Objectives:

- Identify the 4 mindsets that reflect the level of commitment employees have for their employer, which drives them to ask the question, "Do I still want to work here?"
- Discover the 2 stages that every employee goes through to become a productive member of any organization and how critical a positive employee experience within these stages is to retaining them.
- Learn the 5 *Retention Architecture* initiatives that strategically change the culture of trust, communication, and engagement within your company for elevated profits and talent retention.
- Calculate the cost of replacing employees at every position in your organization through the use of Colene's *Turnover Calculator*. This cost information increases HR's power to persuade the C-Suite to adopt initiatives that retain employees, making the company more profitable.

Book Colene at: www.ColeneRogers.com

HUMAN CAPITAL CONSULTING

As a Senior Certified HR professional (SHRM- SCP) and previous talent acquisition manager, Colene understands firsthand the challenges business owners and leaders deal with every day. With human capital consulting, Colene focuses on employment law, hiring, retention, employee engagement, and best policies and practices that come into play as employees perform the day-to-day operations of their organization. She provides employers with solutions that result in measurably improved employee and organizational performance while minimizing employment practice risk. Colene and her team of HR professionals are available to assist the client to identify needs, develop an action plan, and facilitate change to enhance the success of their organization.

Below are just a few examples of where Colene Rogers and Associates can help!

- Turnover Rate and Cost Analysis
- Proper Personnel Classification (exempt vs non-exempt)
- Employee Relations Guidance
- Employee Handbook Development or Review
- Personnel Files Guidelines
- I-9 and E-Verify Compliance
- Policy Development
- Onboarding Program
- Job Description Development or Review
- Interview & Hiring Practices
- Employment Application Forms
- Change Management
- HR Staff Structure & Placement
- Time and Attendance Practices and Records

And much more…

Consult with Colene at: www.ColeneRogers.com

Sign up for a FREE 30-minute consultation to see how her team can help give you peace of mind regarding your Human Resource legal compliance and governmental regulations.

Thank you for reading
Retention: Key Mindsets That Retain Top Talent

To order more copies go to:
www.ColeneRogers.com

Contact Colene for special
bulk discounts for your audience!

Don't forget to claim your **FREE Gift!**

 The Turnover Calculator:
at www. ColeneRogers.com

How to learn the true high cost of turnover per
position.
For client references and more resources on how to
find, retain, and engage your talent visit:

www.ColeneRogers.com

Colene ROGERS
SPEAKER · AUTHOR · CONSULTANT

Colene blends storytelling with business principles for specific, actionable ideas to help you find, retain, and engage talent. Colene is a Senior Certified HR professional (SHRM-SCP), a certified speaker, trainer, and coach with the John Maxwell Team; a certified trainer for Vital Smarts Crucial Conversations and a professional member of the National Speakers Association.

BRING COLENE TO YOUR NEXT EVENT FOR CUSTOMIZED RETENTION SOLUTIONS

Keynote Speaker	Team Building	Conflict Management Training
Executive Coaching	HR Consulting	Leadership Training

WAYS TO STAY CONNECTED WITH COLENE

- 🌐 colenerogers.com
- ✉ colene@colenerogers.com
- 🐦 ColeneSpeaks
- 📷 Colene.Rogers1
- 📘 ColeneRogersSpeaker
- 💼 ColeneRogers

CPSIA information can be obtained
at www.ICGtesting.com
Printed in the USA
LVHW081548130621
690117LV00014B/65

9 781951 492977